THE BLACK SUITCASE MYSTERY™
A WORLD WAR II REMEMBRANCE

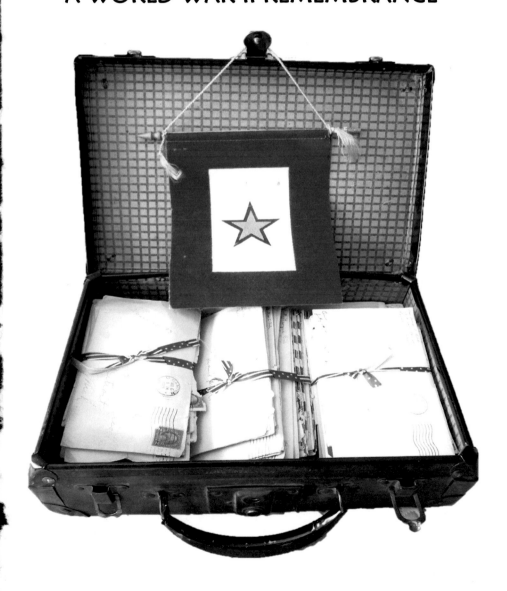

CAST OF CHARACTERS

STAR OF THE STORY: The Black Suitcase

SUPPORTING CAST:

Hazel Elliott Rich
George Elliott Rich
Wanda Bee Rich Dilley

DETECTIVES: Fifth Grade Students at Mark Twain Elementary School in Brentwood, Missouri

1991-1992: 24 Students
1992-1993: 41 Students
1993-1994: 34 Students
1994-1995: 37 Students

ABLE ASSISTANTS: Mark Twain Elementary School Educators. They are "Baby Boomer" daughters of parents who met or married during World War II.

Principal Jackie Whitworth
Librarian Gail Elliott (Thomas) Downs
Fifth Grade Language Arts Teacher Leslie Bran

SETTING

1930-1941: The Great Depression
1941-1945: World War II
1991-1995: 50th Anniversary Commemoration of World War II Events

CREDITS

1991: Television broadcast by local CBS Affiliate; Proclamation given by Missouri House of Representatives; Newspaper coverage in the *St. Louis Post Dispatch*, *West County Journal* and Brentwood *Pulse*.

1992: Recognition in *The United States Congressional Record*; Citicorp Innovative Educator Award; Cable in the Classroom Educator Award; Proclamation from St. Louis County Executive; Article in *456ᵗʰ Bomb Group Newsletter*; Newspaper coverage in the Lancaster, New Hampshire *Coos County Democrat*, St. Louis *Mid-County Suburban Journal*, Brentwood *Pulse* and *Brentwood Public School Bulletin*.

1993: First Elementary School in the United States to be designated a World War II Commemorative Community; A&E Cable Network Educator Award; Proclamation from St. Louis County Executive; Article in *World War II Dispatch*; Newspaper coverage in the *St. Louis Post Dispatch*, *Metro West Post*, Chesterfield *Journal*, Brentwood *Pulse*, *Gateway Reporter* and *Parent Link Newsletter*.

1994: President Bill Clinton commended Mark Twain Elementary School during his Memorial Day Speech at Arlington National Cemetery; Television Broadcasts by local affiliates of NBC and CBS; A&E Cable Network Educator Award; Emerson Electric Corporation Educator Award; Missouri Association of School Librarians "Bright Idea" Award; Newspaper coverage in *USA TODAY*, *St. Louis Post Dispatch*, St. Louis *Mid-County Journal*, St. Louis *West Metro Post*, *Education St. Louis* and *St. Louis Senior Circuit*.

1995: Mark Twain Fifth Graders funded and hosted a 3 day fly-in of the *All American*, a fully restored WWII era B-24 Liberator Bomber; Television coverage by local affiliates of NBC, CBS and ABC; Letter of Commendation from Missouri Governor; Proclamations from Missouri Senate and Missouri House of Representatives; Cable in the Classroom Educator Award; Articles in April issue of the VFW *Veterans of Foreign Wars Magazine* and B-24 Liberator Club *Briefing*; Newspaper coverage in the *St. Louis Post Dispatch*, St. Louis *Mid-County Journal*, St. Louis *West Metro Post*, Webster-Kirkwood *Journal*, Chesterfield *Journal*, *County Star Journal* and Brentwood *Pulse*.

COINCIDENCES IN THE BLACK SUITCASE MYSTERY™

When Gail Elliott (Thomas) Downs first presented the Black Suitcase to the fifth grade students, she had no inkling that the World War II story would reveal an astonishing amount of coincidences as the project developed.

March 21, 1945: Two letters were written on the same day. Wanda wrote Hazel to report George's life insurance policy listed his father Guy as beneficiary. She included Guy's comment after George was listed as Missing in Action, "Guy said he'd never work another day." The Veterans Administration wrote to Wanda the same day, March 21, 1945 and told her she was the actual beneficiary of the $10,000 life insurance payout.

May 1, 1991: Gail, living near St. Louis, Missouri read the letters in the Black Suitcase and discovered a 1944 New York newspaper clipping about George Elliott Rich's B-24 Liberator. The 1944 New York paper reported that the co-pilot was from St. Louis. Contact was made with the local family and Gail was given the exact same article, but from a 1944 St. Louis paper!

May 20, 1991: Two women, George's widow Wanda Bee Rich Dilley in West Virginia and teacher/librarian Gail in Missouri were unknown to each other, but were both linked to the memory of George Elliott Rich. Gail first presented the Black Suitcase to her fifth grade students on Monday, May 20, 1991. Six months later, after contact was made with Wanda, it was discovered that on May 20, 1991 Wanda had written a letter to the BATTLE GROUNDS COMMISSION asking for information about George's grave site.

May 20, 2015: The PROOF COPY of *The Black Suitcase Mystery—A World War II Remembrance* was printed 24 years to the day that fifth grade students first saw the Black Suitcase and Wanda inquired about George's burial location.

December 6, 1991: Pearl Harbor Night at Mark Twain School found two WWII veterans, each a previous guest speaker, attending the program. Both served in the same B-24 squadron in England and flew on the same missions. They hadn't seen each other since 1943.

May 22, 1992: Wanda spoke to the St. Louis fifth graders on what would/should have been her 49th wedding anniversary. Several days later, George's 456th Bomb Group held their 49th reunion in Milwaukee, Wisconsin. Gail and Wanda attended the reunion and met the men who had flown with George during World War II.

June 1992: Wanda and Gail encountered three of George's comrades at the reunion: Jerry Krenek's life was saved by George; Doug Richards was pilot *of Purple Shaft* and George's commander; Wes Hyde flew as co-pilot on mission which killed George and seven other crew members.

December 1992: WWII veteran Richard Verdon, resident of Kalamazoo, Michigan was an eyewitness to George's death. Gail visited relatives in Kalamazoo and met with Dick Verdon during the holidays.

April 1993: Gail discovered that the Tuskegee Airmen of the "Fighting Red Tails" flew their first fighter support mission over Germany on June 9, 1944, with Munich being the target destination. According to the *Purple Shaft's* flight record, the B-24 flew on that same mission to Munich.

December 1993: WWII Infantry Field Nurse June Wandry wrote in her book, *Bedpan Commando*, about visiting her cousin Mike who was in "Steed's Flying Horses". That was correct information, but incorrect designation. June's cousin Mike was really in "Steed's Flying Colts" of the 456th Bomb Group, the same unit as George. June, also a resident of Kalamazoo, Michigan, met with Gail during the 1993 holiday season.

April 1995: Gail asked her local Chamber of Commerce for help raising money to enable the B-24 *All American* to fly into St. Louis. At that function, the Marketing Director from the St. Louis Cardinals Baseball organization was the guest speaker. The Cardinals also wanted to do something to honor WWII Veterans and came on board with the project. The $12,000 would not have been raised without their help.

August 2015: Gail, now a central Oregon coast resident, made contact with Gunther Vogel who has resided on the southern Oregon coast since 1978. Gunther was a 16 year old German gunner assigned to the anti-aircraft battery that shot down George's B-24 on August 22, 1944 over Mechnitz, Poland! A photo of the *Purple Shaft*, on display in a museum in Poland, is identical to one stored in the Black Suitcase since 1944.

Praise for The Black Suitcase Mystery:

"Learning about those times and deeds [World War II] must be more than accidental. Fortunately, many of our fellow Americans understand that. Gail Thomas [now Downs] of Brentwood, Missouri is one of them."
— *President Bill Clinton, "Remarks at a Memorial Day Ceremony in Arlington, Virginia" on May 30, 1994*

"Mrs. Thomas and the fifth-grade students at Mark Twain Elementary serve as models for others to follow in developing and encouraging innovative projects for our children's education."
— *Missouri Senator "Kit" Bond in his remarks for the Congressional Record on May 19, 1992*

Were you an Alabama teacher, you would be my nominee to receive the first award [for teaching history]—and I'm sure you would win!
— *Colonel Robert J. Jakeman, United States Air Force Historical Research Agency and Auburn University Asst. Professor*

"You have shared so beautifully the benefits of your interests and ideas. This is an outstanding project."
— *Dr. Shirley Crenshaw, Professor at Webster University, St. Louis, Missouri*

"What an incredible story! The letters are fascinating!! How extraordinary that you have been able to bring that time alive again through your dad's cousin's life and experiences."
— *Helene Willis, Instructor at Lindenwood University, St. Charles, Missouri*

"The Black Suitcase Mystery is like a social studies lesson going back to the past."
— *Veronica Ramirez, Fifth-grade student, 1992*

"It's like we're living a novel."
— *Joe Sparks, Fifth-grade student, 1995*

THE
BLACK SUITCASE
MYSTERY

A World War II Remembrance

by

Gail Elliott Downs

Cover design:
Krysten Polvado

Cover image:
B-24 Liberator
courtesy of the National Museum
of the United States Air Force, Dayton OH
(Note: Gold Star Banner denotes the death of a military
family member)

Other Images:
Bedpan Commando
courtesy of Elmore Publishing, Holland OH

Photograph of two WWII bombers
courtesy of The Collings Foundation, Stowe, MA

Excerpts:

All excerpts of letters are depicted with
original spelling, grammar, and syntax intact.

Dedication

For two women who lost the love of their lives:
my great-aunt, Hazel Elliott Rich
and
her daughter-in-law Wanda Bee Rich Dilley.

Table of Contents

INTRODUCTION

Introduction

T *he following narrative, which* I refer to as the "The Black Suitcase Mystery" is an incredible, factual and poignant story. It is a timeless tale of love and war, with interwoven threads throughout which are linked in unbelievable ways. What makes the "mystery" in the Black Suitcase story so intriguing is the fact that it was solved by ten year old students over a four year period, 1991-1995.

I, Gail Elliott (Thomas) Downs am the current guardian of a small battered black suitcase which originally belonged to my paternal great-aunt Hazel Elliott Rich. After Hazel's death in 1979, my mother kept the suitcase for three years then gave it to me in 1982. It seems that Hazel originally used the suitcase as a storage container for those special items that mothers hold dear: photographs of their young children, early school papers and handmade cards. However, this small black suitcase is unusual because it holds almost 200 letters and cards mailed in the 1920s, 1930s and 1940s.

Most were written between 1929 and 1942 by Hazel's young son, George Elliott Rich who was living in New Hampshire and writing to his mother in Detroit. Another bundle of George's letters appear to be military in nature dating from 1942 to 1944, then they abruptly stop. Yet a third bundle, written by a feminine hand, begin in 1943 and end in 1946.

After reading some of the letters, several questions came to my mind. Why was George in New Hampshire when his mother was in Detroit? Did they see each other during those 13 years between 1929 and 1942? Why did the military mail suddenly stop? Who wrote the other letters to Hazel?

In the spring of 1991, I was working as the elementary school librarian in Brentwood, Missouri, a bedroom community near St. Louis. A fifth-grade teacher asked if I had anything in the library that might get her students interested in genealogy. I remembered the black suitcase and suggested the students might learn the basics of genealogy by reading the family documents stored within it. With the school year about to end, we agreed to have her students come to the library for extra research sessions the last two weeks in May.

What started, in May 1991, as a way to introduce fifth-grade level students to the basics of genealogical research eventually developed into a four-year study which commemorated the 50th Year Anniversary of numerous World War II events. The idea of introducing young students to a "hands on" genealogical experience involving primary source documents, library resources and even more importantly, the living resources in the community, quickly escalated into a "hearts on" experience of significant historical and personal value for each participant as well.

In late May, 1991 the Black Suitcase was opened and its contents explored by fifth graders for the first time. Although they were exposed to the "mystery" of the old letters for just two weeks, the interest and enthusiasm from the original group of students was heartwarming. I knew I had something unique in that small battered suitcase of letters written by my dad's cousin more than a half century earlier.

I approached Jackie Whitworth, the principal of Mark Twain Elementary School, and told her I had a "gold mine" in that Black Suitcase. I related the excitement the students felt as they examined the letters, especially those written during World War II. I then proposed that we continue the study during the upcoming autumn and plan an event in December, 1991 to commemorate the 50th Anniversary of the attack on Pearl Harbor. Jackie gave her consent, with the stipulation that Leslie Brann, the fifth-grade teacher, agreed to work with me. From that humble beginning, the project grew in unforeseen and astonishing ways, gaining local, state and national recognition before it ended four years later.

During the 1991-1992 school year: the students investigated the contents of the Black Suitcase, found and met the B-24 Liberator bomber pilot revealed in the World War II military mail, hosted a World War II Night on December 6th to commemorate the 50th Anniversary of Pearl Harbor, accepted a Proclamation from the Missouri House of Representatives, received a national education award, were included in the United States Congressional Record and located the female author of the 50-year-old letters in the suitcase.

The next year, 1992-1993: the students read about the "The Black Suitcase Mystery" on the front page of a New Hampshire newspaper published on Veterans Day, helped Mark Twain Elementary School became *the first elementary school in the nation* to be designated as a World War II Commemorative Community, participated in the national Valentines for Vets initiative, produced a video about the Black Suitcase which was shared with several St. Louis regional VA Hospitals, developed relationships with fifth-grade pen-pals in New Hampshire, received a second national education award and learned of a connection involving the Tuskegee Airmen and their triumphs during World War II.

In the third year of the project, 1993-1994: the students hosted a St. Louis Tuskegee Airman on Veterans Day, continued with the Valentines for Vets program, received a third national education award, prepared an evening program to commemorate the 50th Anniversary of D-Day, read about their accomplishments in an issue of the *USA Today* newspaper and heard President Bill Clinton cite their endeavors in his Memorial Day speech at Arlington National Cemetery!

During the last year of the project, 1994-1995: the students were invited to march in the Battle of the Bulge Parade held in St. Louis during the national and international 50th Year Commemoration of that battle, accommodated a World War II Army nurse who was a veteran of the Battle of the Bulge, accepted proclamations from both the Missouri Senate and Missouri House of Representatives, received a fourth national education award, participated in a long-distance celebration of the Victory in Europe 50th Year Commemoration held in Berlin, Germany and finalized fundraising plans that enabled a fully restored B-24 Liberator bomber to fly into St. Louis for a three day commemoration event.

The April 1995 issue of the *Veterans of Foreign Wars Magazine* printed a two page article about the accomplishments of the Mark Twain Elementary School fifth-grade classes who had studied the World War II era. When asked to elaborate on what had transpired during the previous four years, fifth-grade teacher Leslie Brann, wrote:

> In the beginning, neither of us could have predicted the astounding course that this project would follow. Gail's ideas on paper quickly took on even broader meanings than she had originally envisioned. On more than one occasion we have verbalized to each other that something powerful has been at work here! Resources have kept materializing in wondrous and

appropriate ways. Gail has found superb methods for incorporating them into her original plans, and all the while preserving the attitude of "ownership" in the children and myself. In a short time WE became an extension of Gail's family tree as we learned more and more of the era of the World War II flyer whose letters initiated the project in Gail's mind.

Visualize several classes of "cool" fifth graders early in the school year, brought into our library for a specially scheduled library "project" time. What possible interest could some old letters from someone else's dead relative hold for them? What could possibly entice them to spend hour after hour immersed in reference books, aviation manuals, and fiction stories about children who lived in The Forties? Who would believe they would learn the "jitterbug," much less demonstrate it in public? Why would so many of the video generation sit raptly listening to silver-haired veterans telling stories based on events of fifty or more years ago? All of this has led to wonderful history exhibitions prepared by our fifth graders as a Memorial Day Tribute each spring, with the library serving as the focal point of the productions.

That 1995 VFW magazine article concluded with my thoughts:

The program has been an ever-evolving thing. It's been a surprise to everyone that something that started out so small developed into so many areas. Yes, it will be a letdown when it ends. The lives of our WWII veterans have touched me so deeply. These people to me are forever young.

Twenty-five years have now passed and I still marvel at the experiences I shared with the Mark Twain Elementary School staff and fifth-grade students during the 50th year commemoration of World War II events, 1991-1995. When I think back, even earlier to 1982 and my first encounter with the Black Suitcase, I am reminded of how narrowly the suitcase escaped destruction at the hands of my mother.

Three years earlier, while teaching in Germany, I received word that my great-aunt Hazel had died. During the summer of 1980, I flew home and met my mother in Colorado, then drove her back to Detroit to settle the family's estate. Hazel's neighbors had gathered family photographs and mementoes, including the Black Suitcase, and put them in a large steamer trunk for safe keeping. I took Mom and the steamer trunk back to Colorado, then returned to teach in Germany for another two years.

By 1982, I was back in the States living and teaching in St. Louis, Missouri. Plans were made to spend Christmas in Colorado, something I had been unable to do for five years while teaching overseas. On Christmas Eve, a blizzard struck and everyone was house-bound. My mother went to a closet and then handed me the small battered suitcase. She said, "Take this back to St. Louis or I'm going to pitch it. I'm tired of having this old thing hang around here." It had been in her bedroom closet for the past three years.

I had time, on that snowy Christmas Eve of 1982, to read the old letters, so I began. I was uncomfortable in the time-warp I experienced when I read them. It soon felt as though I was intruding in the private lives of others, so I stopped. However, I knew I couldn't have it "pitched" by Mom. It had obviously been cherished by my great-aunt because she had kept it for so many years. I couldn't allow it to be thrown in the trash, but I didn't know what to do with it. I brought it back home to St. Louis and put it into my own bedroom closet where it rested for another nine years, until May of 1991 when it was opened for the fifth-grade students.

Today, when I remember the events I shared with the fifth graders, the remarkable people we met and the accolades we received, all because of the small battered Black Suitcase, I know Mom gave me an incredible gift on that Christmas Eve of 1982!

The reader is invited to join me as I recount the experiences and discoveries made by the Mark Twain fifth-grade students during their four year study of World War II. The first section entitled "Letters from a Lifetime" will explore the contents of the Black Suitcase. The second and third segments are intertwined. The second section, entitled "Fifth Graders Focus on the Forties" relates the events experienced by the students over the four years of 1991-1995. During that time, the students discovered the identity of the woman who wrote the letters dated from 1943 to 1946. The third section which the students called "Where's Wanda?" will be explained in its chronological position within the second section.

For the past twenty or more years, whenever I reflect on all the events that the Mark Twain fifth-grade students and staff commemorated during the 50th Anniversary of World War II, I feel proud of our accomplishments. The current year is 2015 and those ten year old students, who were fifth graders during 1991-1995, are now thirty-five year old adults. I find it hard to believe that so many years have passed. The educators who were involved with the project are now close to the age of the veterans honored twenty-five years ago.

Soon, our nation will be observing and commemorating the 75th Anniversary of World War II. It is my hope that the glimpses into a pivotal and momentous period of America's history, derived from the letters found in the Black Suitcase, will be found as intriguing to today's citizens as they were twenty-five years ago.

1921-1946
LETTERS
FROM A LIFETIME

Letters from a Lifetime

The contents of the Black Suitcase relate to the life of George Elliott Rich, son of Guy A. Rich and his wife, Hazel Elliott Rich. The earliest document in the Black Suitcase is the birth announcement for George, born September 12, 1921. *(Fig. 1)* His maternal grandparents, Mr. and Mrs. C. P. Elliott were the recipients of the birth announcement. It is followed by George's christening photo and another of George at 9 months old with his mother. *(Fig. 2 – 3)* George and Hazel are again pictured together in 1928, when George was in 1ˢᵗ grade. *(Fig. 4)* As a 2ⁿᵈ grader in 1929-1930, George attended two different schools in the Detroit Public System. During the summer of 1930, major changes occurred within the family and George found himself uprooted from the life he knew in Detroit.

Hazel developed tuberculosis in that year and was sent to the Maybury Sanitarium in Northville, Michigan. Maybury Sanitarium served people who were diagnosed with TB at a time

Figure 1: Birth announcement for George Elliott Rich, received by his maternal grandparents Clarence and Amanda Elliott, residents of Detroit, Michigan 1921

when there was no real cure for the disease. The sanitarium was a quarantine and recovery center for Detroit's highly infectious tuberculosis patients. George's father, Guy, was a musician in a traveling band and was unable to care for his young son, so George, with the help of the Traveler's Aid Society, was sent to his grandparents in Lancaster, New Hampshire. *(Fig. 5)* Guy's parents, George and Viola Rich, owned a meat market at 46 Main Street in Lancaster and agreed to care for young George until Hazel's health improved. George enrolled at the local school and started third grade in September, 1930.

By this time, the entire country was impacted by the Great Depression and it is evident from the 90 letters and cards, sent

Figure 2: George's christening portrait taken in Hamilton, Ontario Canada

Figure 3: Nine month old George with his mother Hazel Elliott Rich, Hamilton, Ontario Canada 1922

Figure 4: George and Hazel in Detroit, Michigan 1928

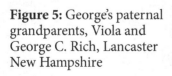

Figure 5: George's paternal grandparents, Viola and George C. Rich, Lancaster New Hampshire

between 1930 and 1942, that George spent his entire childhood and youth in New Hampshire. His grandparents made sure that he kept in touch with his mother regularly. *(Fig. 6)* In the early years, George included spelling and arithmetic quizzes along with handmade Valentines and Mother's Day cards in his letters to Hazel. *(Fig. 7)* He often wrote that he was being a good boy and always sent love to his "Grandma and Uncle Widdie" who were family members taking care of Hazel. On

Figure 6: Sample of childhood letters George wrote to Hazel while living in Lancaster, New Hampshire

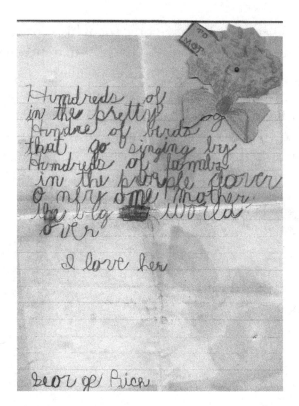

Hundreds of
in the pretty
Hundre of birds
that go singing by
Humdreds of famlys
in the purple cover
O nery one Mother
The big World
over

I love her

George Rice

Figure 7: Handwritten Mother's Day card mailed to Hazel 1931

January 29, 1932 he wrote, "Don't worry, mother, I won't forget you. I'm too big of a boy to forget his mother."

Being a young boy, away from home, he hoped to have the comfort of his favorite toy train. In the very first letter he sent to Hazel in September of 1930 he wrote, "I want you to send my train, please." In March of 1931 he said, "I miss my train a lot. I wish you would please send it." In December of 1932 he wrote, "Please mother, send my train. I miss it so. I have got a dandy place for it." Finally, in June of 1933, he wrote, "Gee mother, I was glad to get my train. I have had a good time with it. But I cannot run it without the transformer. Did you forget to put it in?"

A probable explanation for the long delay in sending his train would be Hazel's continuing battle with tuberculosis.

George did not specifically mention Hazel's health in his earliest letters. However, in August 1935 when he was almost 14, he wrote, "I am sorry to hear that you are sick again. I hope you get well quick. A year or more seems an awful long time in the hospital." On February 10, 1936 he wrote, "I hope the doctor gave you good news about the lungs." In late March he wrote again, "I am sorry to hear that you are not feeling good. I know it isn't much fun to stay in bed and worse in the summer when you can't get out." On June 21 he added, "I am glad you are not any worse than you are. I hope you don't have to stay in bed another year." In November, 1936 he wrote, "I hope you get out of the hospital by next summer. It isn't so bad to stay there during the winter, but it isn't so good to stay in there during the summer." On June 10, 1937 he wrote, "It's too bad you have to stay in the sanitarium all the time and I hope you'll be able to get out of there this summer. It must be dreadful staying in there all summer." In July he again wrote, "I hope you can get out of there before August. If it's as hot out there as it has been here, it must be awful in the hospital." On October 9, 1937, George wrote, "I received your card and picture and I thank you for it. I think the picture is very good of you. *(Fig. 8)* I hope you are much better and can get out soon. How long have you been there? It seems as though you've been there three or four years." At the end of October he wrote again, "I'm sorry to hear you had mastoids. What kind of hospital is it that you're in, where you can get an infection? I certainly hope you can be out of there by Christmas. I guess I'd go crazy if I had to stay in one place so long." His letter of January 7, 1938 said, "I'm glad you were able to be up on Christmas anyway and I hope you get out this spring." In April of 1938, George wrote, "I'm glad you're back home and I bet you are too. I'll be glad when you really get well." Two months later on June 21, 1938 he wrote, "Well, I hope you stay out of the hospital for good. I hope you recover and get well in a hurry."

Figure 8: Hazel as a patient in the Maybury Tuberculosis Sanitarium, Northville, Michigan 1930s

Occasionally, George's grandmother would write to Hazel and those letters give a glimpse of their life during the Depression. On January 2, 1934, Viola Rich wrote, "Business in the meat market is very dull. Not much doing in this small town. What business there is, the chain stores get. I don't think times would be as hard, if it wasn't for so many chain stores and autos. They get all the money there is."

Later that same month, both George and his grandmother sent additional letters to Hazel. George wrote, "I am glad you liked the picture, but sorry it made you cry. Cheer up, Mother. When times get better, I'll get out to see you or you can get up this way. Mother, you couldn't send anything better than the two dollars, as I have five dollars now for a new suit this spring. I want long pants." *(Fig. 9)* His grandmother wrote, "Now don't worry about Georgie, for he has good care. Of course you miss him and would love to see him, and he would love to see you. But keep up your courage. When this terrible depression is over, Guy will probably take him to see you. But as times are now, we are lucky to have a warm place to live and plenty to eat, when so many are hungry and cold."

In 1932, unfortunately, but not surprisingly, George's father Guy and Hazel divorced. George had been away from Hazel for almost two years by then and in his April 1932 letter he wrote, "I wish I could see you mother." In September 1932, George wrote, "Sorry I couldn't visit you this past summer because

Figure 9: George wearing his first suit with long pants, Lancaster, New Hampshire 1934

daddy didn't have the money. But daddy said I could when he could afford the money." The following June 1933 he wrote "Daddy can't afford to let me come out there." On January 2, 1934 George asked, "How about sending me a picture of you? I would like to have one because I have none." The next month he asked, "By the way, when is your birthday? I always wanted to know. Don't forget the picture. I want to know what you look like." On May 21, 1934 George wrote, "Received your letter and pictures and want to thank you for them. I can't tell if I can get out to see you this summer as money is pretty scarce in New Hampshire. But you can't tell what may turn up as I may get to see you sometime soon." In July 1934 he wrote, "I think maybe next summer Dad can manage to let me get out to see you. Money has been scarce this summer and last winter, too." Attempts to see Hazel are not mentioned again until June 10, 1937 when George wrote, "We're going to try to get out to Ohio this summer and Dad's going to try to get me out to see you, but don't plan on it. It's pretty hard for dad to get away from his work."

Although George remained in Lancaster with his grandparents during the early Depression years, Guy had been awarded legal custody of his son after the divorce. In 1935 George, age 14, joined his father who had remarried and now lived in Manchester, New Hampshire. George continued to send greeting cards and letters *(Fig. 10)* to his mother and sometimes commented on events happening in the country. On November 2, 1936 he wrote, "There isn't any school Tuesday because of the election. I hope Roosevelt gets elected again. Who do you want for President?" On July 6, 1937 he wrote, "I went up to Pittsburgh, N. H. with Uncle Earl. We took Cousin Chester up to the C. C. C. camp. It's up by the first Connecticut Lake and you're right in the wilderness up there."

George occasionally mentioned his hobby of building model airplanes. On May 21, 1934 he wrote, "Tell Grandma and Uncle Widdie I said hello, and Cousin Don, too. So Don likes aviation? I do too, but I can't make model planes very well." His next mention of planes was on August 3, 1935 just before starting eighth grade. "I am interested in aviation and am building airplanes. A friend of mine and myself are building an airport for model airplanes. I want to join the Navy and be a flyer when I get out of high school. Of course, I might not feel the same 5 years from now." Then, in late November George wrote, "The plane I am sending you is a model of a regular big one. I just got another plane, the F-35 Beechcraft flying model.

Figure 10: Sample of letters written during George's high school years, Manchester, New Hampshire

I would send you this one only I'm afraid it wouldn't be all together by the time you got it. I was thinking of building a 6 foot model of the Curtiss Robin only the motor cost too much and the wing span is six feet! Some wing span, eh?" George's next letter was dated January 5, 1936 and he shared, "I got so many air planes for Christmas. A total of 14 models to build. I've three built and hanging up in my bedroom. I am working on a Fokker D VIII, a plane used by the Germans in the world war." On March 22, 1937 he wrote, "Right now I'm building a

5 foot Stinson Reliant air liner for another boy. I also built him a Curtiss Robin and a Fokker D VII wartime plane used by the Germans." George's letter of October 9, 1937 said, "I've got a plane I'm going to send you if I ever get it fixed. It's a Fokker D7. Its landing gear got washed out when it came in a little too hard, but I'll have it looking like new again. This type of plane was used by the Germans during the world war. It was the fastest plane in the world then, attaining the terrific speed of 126 M. P. H. I'll get it off to you as quick as I can."

Photographs taken during this time show George growing into a tall, handsome young man. *(Fig. 11)* In his November 8, 1938 letter he wrote, "Just think, I'm beginning to shave, must be getting old." His letter of February 17, 1939 shared details about a dance:

Figure 11: George with one of several wire-haired fox terrier dogs the family owned

Next Monday night the Pro Christo Society of the church I go to is having a semi-formal dance. I'm taking a girl who is going to her first formal dance. Well, for that matter, so am I.

In his May 30, 1939 letter George wrote:

I had a swell time at that dance and last Friday I went to the Junior Prom. We did things up in real style by having it at the Manchester Country Club and boy what a swanky joint. All the Big Shots here in town belong to it. Dad took the girl and me out and brought us back. At the intermission, a boy I knew and his girl took us up to the Howard Johnson's which is a big place out of town a few miles. We got back just in time for the last dance. We sure did have a lot of fun. Last night I was invited up to the girl's house, whom I took to the Prom, for supper. Incidentally, it was her birthday so I took her a box of chocolates. Her mother gave me enough money to take her to the show at the State, which is the best theater here in town. We saw *Union Pacific*.

As a high school student, George participated in school sports and worked part-time in a local drug store. Most of his letters tell of his class work, grades and football games on the weekends. He had a good voice and was a member of the school chorus. His high school had established the custom of staging Gilbert & Sullivan operettas and George participated in three productions: *The Mikado, Yeomen of the Guard* and *Iolanthe*. In his February 1939 letter, George reported, "We just had a successful showing of the operetta Yeomen of the Guard and the second night we had over 1,400 people which was a full house." *(Fig. 12)*

Figure 12: George as a cast member in a high school operetta "Yeoman of the Guard" 1939

There are three items in the Black Suitcase that make the reader wonder about George's relationship with his father during his high school years.

On July 29, 1938 Hazel received a telegram from Guy which said, "Please wire me immediately if George shows up at Detroit or if [you] hear of him." *(Fig. 13)* The rough draft of Hazel's telegram back to Guy said, "George not here yet. How long has he been gone. Did he have any money. Also wire if he returns and please write me details." Chronologically, the next item in the Suitcase is another rough draft. It was of a letter Hazel wrote to Guy on November 3, 1938:

I've been wondering over this long silence on George's part. Is he ill? I can hardly believe that because, surely, you would have let me know. We've been parted long enough to forget personal animosity, or are you still motivated by that feeling for revenge and a desire to force an acknowledgement of your superiority? If you are, you might as well forget it. You'll be the loser in the long run. I've written George today, too. Can it be possible that anything concerning last summer is keeping him from writing? I can't understand why that should. ~~I suppose there is no use asking you to relieve my anxiety about him. If he has just been forgetful,~~ I Certainly you should know by now that what you do, or what you are, or why, are of no interest

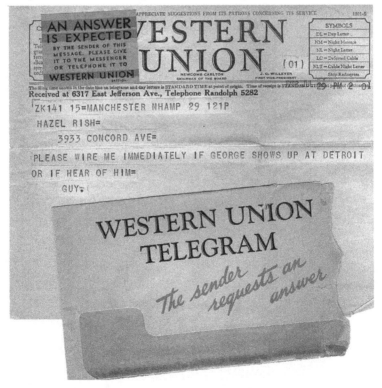

Figure 13: Telegram George's father sent to Hazel 1938

to me anymore. I have no desire to intrude upon your ~~affairs~~ life. All I want is to keep in touch with George. After all, he's mine, too. If he has just been neglectful, prod him a little, will you? And if it is anything more serious, please let me know. That's only fair.

A few days later, on November 8, 1938 George wrote:

I hope you will forgive me for not writing to you sooner. It's terrible hard for me to sit down and write a letter. As far as that affair is concerned last summer, don't let it worry you. I guess I was only out for a little adventure and I'm sorry it caused everyone so much worry. I assure you, it won't happen again.

George's remaining letters written during his high school years give no details relating to the "adventure" he had during the summer of 1938. On May 7, 1940 George wrote:

Well there is less than a month of school left for me now. I graduate in June and boy do I hate to get out. Last September I was elected Home Room representative. I got my part in the operetta and boy what fun. I have a couple of pictures here that I'm going to send you where I was working last summer. *(Fig. 14 – 15)* I am going back to work in Maine this summer, so after the 4th my address will be the same as last summer."

George had worked at the Chapman House Inn, a small guest hotel near the beach in Ogunquit Maine. Information from an early brochure advertised the "CHAPMAN HOUSE, N.F. Chapman, Prop. Littlefield Corners, Ogunquit, Me."

Figure 14: George on a break from his summer job at the Chapman House Inn, Ogunquit, Maine 1939

Figure 15: George and a friend on the grounds of the Chapman House Inn, Ogunquit, Maine

The Chapman House is a great favorite because every effort is made to thoroughly satisfy its guests. The rooms are pleasant and comfortably furnished, the bill of fare appeals successfully to all varieties of taste, the cooking is always good and every effort is made to assure the comfort and amusement of patrons. The rates are so reasonable as to be well within the means of the average family, and it should require no further explanation why the Chapman House is an established favorite.

An automobile is run in connection with the house, which carries passengers and baggage from depot and return. It may also be engaged for pleasure riding (a careful driver is in charge). Trolley cars pass the door. The house accommodates twenty-five, but several cottagers are table guests.

In his July 13, 1940 letter, he commented:

I'm working here at the same place I did last year. I had quite a time with graduation and everything you know. I really did graduate. It's a wonder with the marks I got. I trust you got the picture okay. *(Fig. 16)* We have had pretty tough weather so far this summer. I've been here going on 3 weeks and we have had about 3 days without rain.

George's next letter, written on July 23, 1940 said:

From the letter head I guess you can see that I'm still at the Chapman House. *(Fig. 17)* As I write this letter, I'm sitting at the desk to see that all the guests are OK. Tuesday and Thursday nights are the regular fellow's night off so I have to stay up and see that

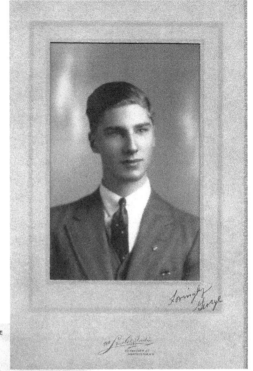

Figure 16: George's high school graduation portrait June 1940

CHAPMAN HOUSE
Shore Road
Ogunquit - Maine
MRS. R. W. CHAPMAN, MANAGER

July 23, 1940
Ogunquite, Me.

Dear Mother,
I got your letter the other day
and was sure glad to he...
you probably got my ...
letter head ...
I'm still at ...

G. E. Rich
Chapman Ho...
Ogunquit, ...

OGUNQUIT, MAINE
JUL 24
1940

Hazel Rich
12108 Chelsea
Detroit, Mich.
U.S.A.

... wrote to let
you ... your letter ok.
I'm gla... liked the picture. I didn't
think th... were so hot.
Well I'll close now with love
& kisses. Give my love to Uncle
Waddie & Grandma.
Love George

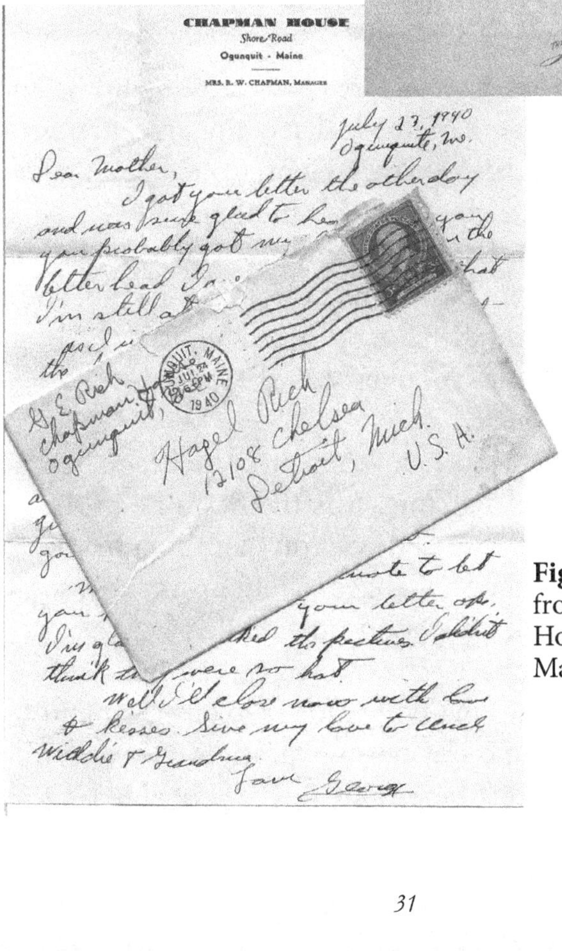

Figure 17: Letter written from the Chapman House Inn, Ogunquit, Maine July 1940

things are locked up. We have about 35 guests now. How long it's going to last, I don't know.

After graduation and the summer in Ogunquit, George enrolled at the Hessar's Business College in Manchester where he attended night school two evenings a week. On December 2, 1940 he wrote:

> I sent for my birth certificate as I needed it to join the Navy. I went down and passed all exams, but Dad talked me out of it, so I went out and got a job instead. I guess that's better. I am going to start work sometime this month in a chicken hatchery. They hatch chicks by the thousands and send them out a day old. My job is to keep a watch on the incubators and drive a one ton truck around.

It had been 10 years since George left Detroit, and he and Hazel had not seen each other during that entire time. In several of his letters over the next two years, George once again talked about getting back to Detroit to see his mother.

In his December 2, 1940 letter he wrote, "Maybe I'll be able to get out next summer if I buy a car. I don't know. I'm not going to make any promises and then not be able to fulfill them." More than a year later, he wrote on January 29, 1941:

> I have permanent work now here in Manchester. I'm working at the drug store. It is the best one in the city. The reason why dad wouldn't let me join the navy was that later on I'll have to join up anyway, so I might as well have a good time while I can. Next summer sometime I get a two week vacation with pay. So right now I'm saving money to buy a car and maybe I can come out on my vacation. Of course the car I buy won't be a Rolls Royce probably be a

Model A Roadster but as long as it gets me out there that's all I care. I guess it's been almost eleven years since I have seen you so I really will make an effort, but I can't promise.

On September 10, 1941, he wrote:

I've got my so called 'horseless carriage' and boy what a car. Maybe I told you about it. Anyway, I'll tell you again. It's a 1931 Pontiac Coupe with rumble seat and all. *(Fig. 18)* I only paid $30 for it, but it

Figure 18: George with his first car, a 1931 Pontiac Coupe, Manchester, New Hampshire 1941

really is a buy. I've had it since April. I wouldn't be afraid to go to California with it. Next summer I hope to be able to come out as I will have two weeks' vacation with pay. Gosh, it's hard to believe, but I'll be twenty in a couple of days and in another year 21, boy oh boy, does time fly. Say you ought to see our airbase here. Is it a humdinger [with] all kinds of soldiers, planes and stuff, but I'll stick to the U.S. Navy, our first line of defense.

Just three months later, America was at war with Germany and Japan. George does not specifically mention the December 7, 1941 bombing of Pearl Harbor, but it might have been on Hazel's mind. George's letter to her, written on January 4, 1942 began:

Gee whiz, you sound like you weren't ever going to see me again. Not if I can help it. I want to quit my job and come out this winter if I can get enough money together. It would cost me about $12 in gas and oil for the car but I want to take along about $50. My tires are good and it's in pretty good shape.

In the post script to that letter, he wrote:

From now on, I wish you would send your letters to 1077 Elm St. Manchester c/o C. D. Tufts [the drug store address]. In that way, Dad won't know what's up as I don't think he wants me to come.

The next letter in the Black Suitcase was written on May 8, 1942:

I've registered for the draft and got a fairly high number but they have lowered it quite a lot. You can bet your boots I won't be called for army service.

I'm going to join the Marines first. I suppose you people are laughing at us here in the east for gas rationing and blackouts and so forth, but I'm telling you it's serious. 2 or 3 gallons a week isn't much. And the blackout is frightening when a whole city goes black and you can't see a finger ¼ inch away from your eye and I'm not kidding, it really is black. The whole seacoast is dimmed out. You can only drive with parking lights on, boy you can't go very fast that way.

Two weeks later, on May 22, 1942 George wrote:

Well hold onto your hat if you wear one because I'll see you the 14th or 15th of June. I'm saving up my gas and am going to drive right straight thru. I'm also getting some extra gas. About 25 gals I'm going to carry with me, plus what my tank holds. I hope I can buy gas out your way. You see I want to come in June before they start rationing out your way. Keep your fingers crossed.

The next week, on May 30, 1942 he wrote:

I'm leaving here early Sunday morning the 14th and I'm going to try and go straight through. If I can I'll be at your place in 20 hours. I'm leaving at three in the morning. Now here is what I want you to do. I'll be coming in from Toledo, Ohio on Route 25. I want a diagram or map on how to get to your house because you know Detroit is a big town. And have Uncle Widdie dig up two or three 5 gal cans because I'm going to need them coming back because my ration card will be all gone and I'll have to carry lots of gas with me on the way back. I'll only be able to stay a week because I have some friends I want to visit in Ohio. Don't forget the map.

George arrived safely in Detroit for a reunion with his mother. Hazel had not seen her son since 1930 when he left for New Hampshire as an eight year old boy. *(Fig. 19 – 20)* George stayed just a week, then sent a postcard from Canton, Ohio on June 20, 1942 and said, "Got here at Canton at 11 AM. Just about 7 hrs. Made it oke. More later."

The Suitcase contains another rough draft of a letter Hazel composed that same day, June 20, 1942. It gives an indication of how she felt being with her son after so many years apart:

Figure 19: George's visit with Hazel, Detroit, Michigan June 1942

Figure 20: Hazel with George's car, Detroit, Michigan

George Dear,

I'm sitting here all alone. I don't want to go back to bed. I want to try to keep myself from dwelling on the fact that you are gone almost before I could really realize you were here. I never thought I'd be shy or a little uncertain of my actions or words towards you. But I guess all these years I subconsciously thought of you as my little boy whom I love so deeply there has never been room for anyone else. I knew you were growing into a splendid young man that I'd always be proud of. But when I was suddenly face to face with you, I was at a loss of words to let you know how I felt. I realized suddenly how I might embarrass you with too much show of love and was also afraid I might not say or do enough. My heart aches with the knowledge that I've missed so much in being deprived of the privilege of living with you as you grew and matured into a young man. But believe me Dear, I'm so proud of you. I've offered a prayer of Thanks every night and shall continue to do so for being your Mother. I want you to know that all my life I will cherish you. I don't want to make you unhappy, George, by these thoughts. On the contrary, I want you to know and be glad in the knowledge that I love you always and forever. Never, never forget it. It may help you sometime when the going gets rough and steep. I want these thoughts to be completely all yours, so I am addressing the envelope to the store.

In his next letter, written on July 10, 1942, George reported:

I got home all oke, with no trouble at all. I got in the back yard and had a flat tire! Some fun. Well, I tried to get in the Marines but they turned me down because I had a slight curvature of the spine, but it's nothing serious. If it hadn't been for that, I would have been in. So I guess I'll have to wait for the army.

His letter dated July 31, 1942 stated:

I got my Induction notice yesterday and I have to report for Induction the 11th of August and probably leave the 25th of August for Fort Devens. That's the Recruit Reception Center where they give you uniforms and etc. Then they ship you some where for training. Boy is Gasoline scarce now. 32 gallons has got to last me two months. I should worry, I'll be in the Army. I'll let you know where I'll be stationed. But don't worry if you don't get a letter from me right away. You see they don't let you write the first two or three weeks your in the army.

In late August of 1942, a month before his 21st birthday, George was a Private in the United States Army. The first military mail that George sent was a postcard with the message, "On my way. Where, I don't know. Will let you know later." *(Fig. 21)* Another postcard was sent from Fort Devens, Massachusetts, *(Fig. 22)* where he had basic training and took an aptitude test which placed him into the Air Corps. At Keesler Field in Biloxi, Mississippi he took more tests and it was determined he would be assigned to the Radio Branch.

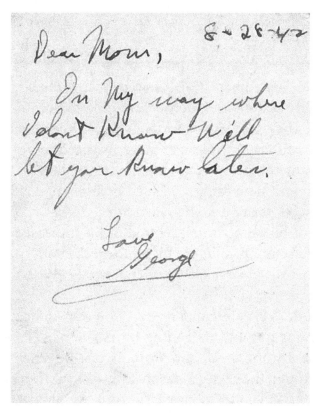

Figure 21: First postcard George mailed to Hazel after joining the Army August 1942

Ready for Company Drill at Fort Devens, Mass.

Figure 22: Postcard mailed from Ft. Devens, Massachusetts during Army Basic Training

By late September 1942 George was stationed in Sioux Falls, South Dakota for extensive training to become a Radio Operator. The course work normally took a year, but had been condensed to just 22 weeks because the need was so great at that time in the war. He commented that the Air Base was another brand new camp and they had lots of mud when it rained, then lots of dust when it was dry.

Most of his letters to Hazel told of his increased speed in taking and sending code. He found the tasks both challenging and frustrating. George's letter of October 12, 1942 said:

> Code is oke, but after a while you start to beat your brains out and its getting on my nerves. I passed the 8 word check and am now on 10. When I got through the check, I was shaking like a leaf so I don't think I'm going to be a very good operator."

His next letter was written on October 21st and he reported:

Well, I'm not so discouraged now. I'm almost thru the first phase. My average is above 90% so I'm not doing so bad. I'm taking 12 words a minute now and sometimes 14 a minute. I expect to get it in a couple of weeks. We have to be able to take 10 words a minute, blinker system, without writing it down. Some fun! [The "blinker light" was an effective tool for spelling out messages in Morse code. It was used to preserve radio silence.]

On December 3rd George wrote:

I finally got on 16 words. I almost passed that the first night except I just missed it by two letters. It's always by one or two, not by a dozen or more. It's so darn aggravating.

When he left Sioux Falls, two months later, he reported:

I got credit for 18 words a minute, code and 10 words a minute, blinker. I worked in the towers for 6 days, sometimes on the high power laison set and then on Blinkers. It was a lot of fun. [The laison set was a radio transmitter that found widespread use during World War II in military aircraft. Under favorable atmospheric conditions communications could be established between aircraft and ground stations separated by thousands of miles.]

During the time George was at the Radio School, Hazel would often send boxes of cookies. He would comment on how good they tasted and how much he and his buddies enjoyed them. *(Fig. 23)* In some of his letters, George told about camp life and the local towns. On November 18, 1942 he wrote:

Boy do we get strong winds up here. I'm telling you it almost blows the Barracks away and I'm not fooling.

Figure 23: Radio School barrack buddies, Sioux Falls, South Dakota 1942

The people here are swell. They take the soldiers right into their homes as one of their own. It sure is easy to hitch hike. I went to town and the first car that came along picked me up and I got a ride right into town. The same way coming back. It sure is wonderful how people treat you out here. We have enough to keep us busy. We have a theater here on the post and we see all the first class pictures for 15¢.

George used a variety of stationery while at school and the Black Suitcase contains several samples of military mail during this period. There is a letter that folds up, making the reverse side an envelope and another with the slogan "Idle Gossip Sinks Ships" printed on the envelope. The mail sent from military posts in the United States during this time had the word "free" written where postage stamps were usually applied. (*Fig. 24 – 25*)

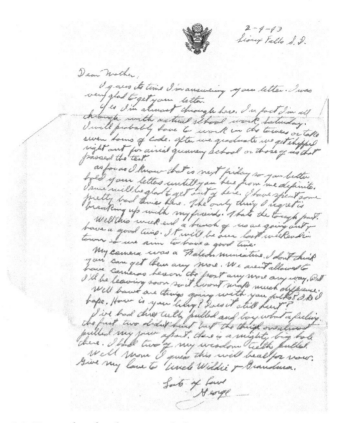

Figure 24: Example of military mail showing stationery which could be folded, thus becoming the envelope as well

Figure 25: Military mail with slogan "Idle Gossip Sinks Ships"

In February, 1943 after five months of Radio School, George was sent to Las Vegas, Nevada for Air Gunnery School. While waiting for the school to start, the men went through more processing. George's letter of February 23, 1943 said:

> Last night we went up to 38,000 feet. Way up in the stratosphere. I took it oke. Some guys got cramps or bends and some got aches in their joints. We all wore oxygen masks. One fellow passed right out and had to go down. All the fellows that got that way are taken down in a separate chamber. This is all done in a pressure chamber. We went up again to 18,000 feet without masks to see what would happen without oxygen. Some got dizzy, others turned blue. We stayed up for 10 or 15 min and then came down. When we came down from 38,000 ft. I thought my eardrums were going to break. There still stopped up.

The first few weeks of the Air Gunnery School were spent in classes on aircraft recognition and familiarity with the 50-caliber machine gun and sights. George thought the courses were very interesting and he earned high grades. He especially enjoyed the times at the firing ranges. He hoped he could do as well in the air.

On March 28, 1943 George wrote:

> Well, I start flying tomorrow. I take off at 11:05 on my first mission. I have to fire from an open cockpit with a flexible 30 cal. machine gun.

The next day, March 29 he wrote:

> Well I went up today for the first time and I wouldn't have missed it for the world. When you're upstairs

it's just like being in another world. It sure is great. I shot out of an open cockpit at about 200 miles an hour. We had to stand up. It was a lot of fun. I looked pretty cute with a flying suit on, helmet and goggles. When we peel off into the target and away from it, it sure is fun. When I get through firing I bang my gun up and down & then hang on. All that holds me in is my gunner's belt. Of course I have a chute on in case anything happens. I only got ten hits out of a hundred rounds. I get two hundred tomorrow. I hope I can do better. All I can say is there is nothing like flying. I was really scared to go up and I was afraid I was going to be sick. But I wasn't and everything came off oke. Everything looks so darn funny from the air. So darn small. All you can see is mountains, desert and sagebrush.

On April 5, 1943 he wrote:

We are shipping out tomorrow. I got my wings and graduated oke. It sure is great flying. There is nothing like it. We got some beautiful equipment, that is, flying clothes.

Five days later, he mailed his next letter from Pocatello, Idaho. Two weeks later, in his April 20, 1943 letter to Hazel, he gave more details about his posting:

I'm a radio operator gunner. If I get to be a chief radio operator, I'll be a T/Sgt. [Technical Sergeant]. If an assistant, I'll be a S/Sgt. [Staff Sergeant] and principally a waste gunner. We got some swell flying clothes. We got a heavy leather sheepskin winter outfit and the jacket I got is an officer's. Its big and really warm. I also got heavy boots. I got a winter and summer helmet with goggles. A May West life preserver in case I land in the water, a pair of $15 sun glasses & a parachute. I was supposed to get a leather summer flying jacket & leather summer flying coveralls. They didn't have my size so I'll get them later. I got a swell case to carry this stuff in too. My wings I wear on my left breast just the same as a pilot. They are silver metal & are the same size but have a different design in the center. I have flown 20 hrs. already this week. Sometimes all night, & then 5 until noon, & then all day. It sure is great.

It is evident from the stack of military mail in the Black Suitcase, consisting of 58 letters, that George was a determined airman and progressed through the ranks quickly. During the first nine months, from his enlistment in August 1942 to June 1943, he was a private, then a corporal, then a sergeant, then back to a private. What happened? *(Fig. 26)*

Figure 26: George's rank increased from Private to Sergeant, then back to Private

George explained the situation in his June 28, 1943 letter to Hazel. However, the Black Suitcase contains some possible clues because there is a photograph of a young couple and a wedding announcement with the information that "Sergeant George Elliott Rich and Wanda Bee, from Parkersburg, West Virginia were married on May 22, 1943 in Pocatello, Idaho." *(Fig. 27 -28)*

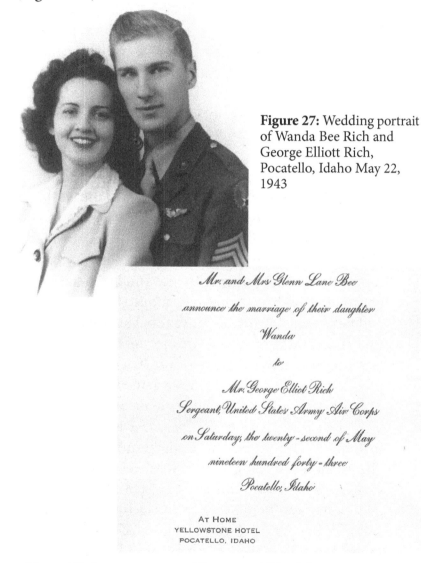

Figure 27: Wedding portrait of Wanda Bee Rich and George Elliott Rich, Pocatello, Idaho May 22, 1943

Mr. and Mrs Glenn Lane Bee

announce the marriage of their daughter

Wanda

to

Mr. George Elliot Rich
Sergeant, United States Army Air Corps

on Saturday, the twenty-second of May

nineteen hundred forty-three

Pocatello, Idaho

AT HOME
YELLOWSTONE HOTEL
POCATELLO, IDAHO

Figure 28: Announcement of George and Wanda's marriage

George first indicated he had a girlfriend in one of his early letters written from Sioux Falls on September 11, 1942. He talked about getting leave after his radio schooling and hoped he could make it back to Detroit. He added, "I also want to stop in Belpre, Ohio [across the Ohio River from Parkersburg West Virginia] and see a certain little party."

On October 12, 1942 he wrote:

> I'm going to get married in a few months. Altho I haven't asked the girl yet. You know, its that girl in W. Va. We sort of have a mutual understanding.

In his next letter, dated October 21, 1942 he added more information.

> I'm very serious in my intention of getting married. I love this girl more than anything else in the world and I'm sure she loves me. She really is one out of a million. She is Dad's wife's sister's husband's niece. She is a very pretty girl and smart. So it isn't just a pretty face that got me. Its the Intelligence that goes along with it. I met her about six years ago and have actually seen her just about six times. The first time and then about 4 times in 1940 & then last summer. [She was one of the 'friends' George mentioned in his May 30, 1942 letter when planning his trip to Detroit. "I'll only be able to stay a week because I have some friends I want to visit in Ohio".] I hope you can understand how I feel. She is the only thing that makes me stay on the straight & narrow altho I think I could do pretty good anyhow. There isn't a day goes by that I don't think of her. There are an awful lot of temptations in the Army, but I want her to be proud of me & I'm going to try my darndest.

On November 10, 1942 he wrote, "I wish I could write more but I've got to drop a line to my girl. I write every day if I can, even if I have to drop everything else."

A week later, on November 18, 1942 George wrote, "My Girl's name now is Wanda Bee but I hope to change it some day. She sure is swell."

Then on November 25th George wrote, "I'm glad you like the picture. I also sent one to Wanda. I thot it came out pretty good, too." *(Fig. 29)*

George didn't mention Wanda again until he was stationed in Pocatello, Idaho. On April 10, 1943 he wrote about their wedding preparations:

Figure 29: Military portrait of George taken while attending Radio School, Sioux Falls, South Dakota 1942

At last I'm done with the technical schools. Now I start my schooling for overseas duty. I'll be here for 3 or 4 months and I won't get a furlough so the report goes. I was going to get married to the girl in W. Va. but I guess I can't now unless she comes out here. Is it a surprise to you? To think I'm going to get married? We have been planning it some time now. I hope she does come out.

Ten days later, on April 20, 1943 he wrote:

I'm having my girl come out here & we are getting married here. I have already bought the ring. I got one for myself also. It cost me $60 smackers. Not much but a lot on a soldier's pay. They really are slick. You can rest assured that my love for Wanda is something that can't be broken up. She feels the same way, too. Its not the War that brought it on. Its been coming on for a long time. I'm not one to say I love a girl & then forget it. I mean it & I'm sure she does.

On May 1, 1943 he commented:

I've been trying to get a room for Wanda but without much success. Its pretty hard to get anything around here especially without money. We get paid pretty soon I hope.

On May 16th George wrote:

I got paid yesterday and I drew $111 cash. Boy, my pockets are loaded down with cash. I've still got to get a room for Wanda. I can get one in one of the smaller towns, but I would rather have her here in town.

After the wedding George wrote a letter dated May 25, 1943 and said:

> Just a short note to let you know you have a daughter-in-law. Wanda and I got married Saturday evening. She got here Sat. noon and we sure had a hectic 24 hrs. getting a license, finding a minister etc. Boy I can hardly believe it myself but it's true. Everything went off pretty smooth.

On June 1, 1943 George wrote:

> I suppose you have my short note about getting married. There isn't much more I can add to that but I can say I'm a very happy man & soldier. It seems awful funny to introduce Wanda as my wife to some of the boys but it's the truth. I love her very much & I know she loves me. Here is Wanda's address if you should want to write her: Mrs. George E. Rich, Room 206, Yellowstone Hotel, Pocatello, Idaho.

Almost a month went by before George wrote again, on June 28, 1943.

> I'm truly sorry for not writing sooner, but there have been certain reasons why I haven't and I will attempt to explain why. The main reason is that I have lost my stripes and was rather ashamed to write. I attempted to leave the post on an illegal pass as we were restricted. I got as far as the gate and my pass was pulled. As a result I lost my stripes, restricted for 30 days & lost a third of my pay for a month. A pretty rough deal but it could have been a lot worse. As a result I have lost three weeks flying

and have been taken off the crew. I would have left on an 8 day furlough this month & I would have been overseas, the next month. Now I will probably start all over again.

After her marriage to George, Wanda began a diligent correspondence with her, as of yet unmet, mother-in-law Hazel. *(Fig. 30)* The Black Suitcase contains 35 letters written by Wanda and sent to Hazel between 1943 and 1946.

Wanda's first letter is dated June 21, 1943 and has a return address of 508 W. Holliday Street, Pocatello, Idaho. She commented:

Figure 30: Samples of letters Wanda wrote to Hazel, her mother-in-law she had yet to meet

Since you and George seem so much alike, I just know I will love you very much, too. George looks grand, he weighs around 150 and seems so healthy. Love is certainly a wonderful thing. We have both been so excited since the 22nd of May, we hardly seem sane. But we enjoy every day as it comes, for time is so short in war . . . As you can see by the address, I have a room in a private home now.

In mid-July, George wrote and said:

Everything is the same here. I hope to start flying again in about two or three weeks. I haven't done anything for almost two months.

A month later, George wrote from Gowen Field near Boise, Idaho:

I'm waiting here to pick up a new crew meanwhile I do a little flying and go to ground school. Wanda has been up here this week, but is going back tomorrow. She is still at the same address in Pocatello.

Wanda wrote her second letter to Hazel on August 24, 1943 and apologized for the long delay between letters. She said:

Three months of married life and no quarrel yet. Ha! We both intend seriously, though, to always keep it this way. We will be so glad when we can have our own home. Here is hoping it won't be too long from now. The war situation seems to be taking a turn for the better.

The next letter in the suitcase is dated October 2, 1943 and George was still a Private, but now assigned to the 746th Bomb

Squadron of the 456th Bomb Group in Muroc, California. He said the base was on the edge of the Mojave Desert, 30 miles from the nearest town, but only 88 miles from Los Angeles. He wrote:

> They gave us a 10 day furlough from Salt Lake City. Of course, I went home. That's where Wanda is now, up in Lancaster.

On October 10, 1943 Corporal George E. Rich wrote:

> Yes, this is the permanent outfit at last. The whole group will move overseas. There are four squads in the group. I sure hope we go to England but you never can tell. We have just about six weeks left before being ready for War. It's kind of a funny thing to say, but it's true. Wanda is staying in Lancaster for the time being. I may have her come to L.A. as I can get in once a week. I sure want to see her again before I leave. She is staying at Grandma Rich's, so it will be the same address. I'm sorry I couldn't get to see you, but hope you understand how things are.

The next letter is dated November 2, 1943 and Wanda wrote:

> Well, like George told you, I am planning to go to L.A. I have been working in a paper mill near Lancaster to save enough for train fare. It took all we could save for our trip east. But I'm going to be with George before the 1st of Dec. and that's all I can think of. I was very sorry that we couldn't see you on our trip — but, hope you can understand. Winter is almost here. The mountains are all covered with snow. I'm glad I won't be here for the bad weather. Lancaster is quite a sleepy little village.

George wrote on November 7, 1943 from Muroc:

> Well, everything is about the same here. The other day we flew 12 hrs. Today we have flown 6 hrs and 20 min. (so far). We have to go up again this evening. It sure is nerve wracking. Boy it is no fun flying at 25,000 ft. Its so darn cold it isn't even funny. If you don't think that we airmen don't work boy think again. And if you ever hear anybody make any smart remarks tell them to join up & find out how tough it is. The other day one of my buddies was walking down the street with his wife (this was in town, not L.A.) and a couple of 4-F civilians or otherwise said, 'There goes one of those damn gunners again.' Boy if that was me and I didn't have my wife with me, I would have laid those guys out in a red plush coffin. There really going after these draft dodgers in L.A. There sure is a lot of them.

George's next letter was written on November 19, 1943 and he said:

> Wanda is out here now. She is staying in N. Hollywood, Calif with some friends. Boy it sure was good to see her again. I really missed her. I can tell you where I am, but not the exact location. That is against army regulations. It won't be too long now before we are gone.

On December 9, 1943 Wanda mailed a Christmas card to Hazel with a return address in North Hollywood, California. She wrote:

> Have spent a month here with George. We've had a wonderful time. George phoned me on December

1st from San Francisco. That was the last time I heard from him. He must be overseas by now. I am leaving in the morning for W. Va. As soon as George sends me his new address, I'll send it to you. Will write a long letter when I'm settled again. This won't be a very happy Christmas for me but it won't be for long.

More than a month passed before Hazel got her next letter from George, written on December 23, 1943. It had a return address of A.P.O. 9203, c/o Postmaster, New York City, New York. That letter and all future letters were stamped indicating they were "Passed by US Army Examiner." The US Examiner was quite often one of George's officers from the flight crew. *(Fig. 31 – 32)*

In that letter, George wrote:

I guess I better write before you start worrying to much. I can't tell you where I am. This is sure going to be a lousy Christmas. I haven't got any mail for a month and probably won't get any for another month. It sure burns me up, but I guess it can't be helped. Of course I haven't heard from Wanda & I'm pretty much worried about her. Of course I can't very well hear from her. I sent her more than enough money to get home and she also got her first allotment. I'm sorry I couldn't call you up, but I didn't want to call up from Calif. as it was too far. After we left Muroc we weren't allowed to call. However we could write letters up until we left Hamilton Field & then we could neither write or call. Its pretty rough but I'm not the only one.

Wanda wrote a letter on December 26, 1943 with a return address in Parkersburg, West Virginia:

Figure 31: Military mail that passed through the squadron's censors, usually the ranking flight officers

Figure 32: Flight officers of the *Purple Shaft*: Pilot Doug Richards, Co-pilot Wilson Goodall, Navigator Robert Thompson and Bombardier Dan Curran

Well, I am at my own home again. George must be overseas by now. I had a letter from him postmarked Dec. 15 in Midland, Texas. But I haven't heard a word since. As soon as I get his address, I'll send it to you. I surely do get lonesome for George. But we've had many good times together and so there are lots of pleasant memories. I'll be glad when his letters begin to come.

New Year's Day of 1944, George wrote:

I hope you had a nice Christmas and New Year's. We are going to have a belated Christmas. As yet, we aren't able to receive mail. I'm sorry I couldn't call you up, but the last month we weren't allowed to telephone or telegraph so I just couldn't, altho I wanted to.

Wanda sent a letter, postmarked January 3, 1944:

I haven't heard another word from George. Wonder where he'll be next. George and I have rather definitely decided on a small home in the country. He has been mingling with such large amounts of this human race around camps. So all we ask is a little peace and quiet. George was promoted to Staff Sergeant after he left Muroc. It must have been between San Francisco and Texas. Try not to worry too much about George. We both feel sure that he'll be back before we realize it. George never looked at it any other way, so neither do I. After all, the optimistic side of life is the best.

Wanda's next letter was dated January 28, 1944:

At last I've heard from George. He is in Tunis, North Africa. They stopped a few days in Brazil on the way over. Apparently, they won't go into combat right away. He hasn't received any of his mail yet. George has a new A.P.O. address: A.P.O. 520 — c/o Postmaster New York City, New York.

George wrote a few days later, on January 31, 1944:

Received your little note with the money. Thanks very much. It was a little late for Wanda & me to have a good time on it, as I'm in N. Africa & she is in Parkersburg. Its pretty nice over here but its cold at night. We had an old German truck that we fixed up to use & we went to town quite often.

His next letter was dated February 4, 1944, Italy:

Everything is oke here except I'm sleeping on the ground. At least I have a big tent. A lot of the boys are living in pup tents. The chow is pretty good considering the handicaps the Mess Sgt. has to go through. He sure does a pretty good job, too. One of the other boys on the crew & I did a little work on our fox hole, but we hit a rock ledge & it sure is hard.

On February 11, 1944 George wrote:

Received your letter of the 27th of Dec. I have received a V-Mail from you since then. I'm glad Wanda called you up. I wrote & asked her to since I couldn't. We have one mission down and forty-nine to go. [During that period of the war, flight crews would rotate back to the United States after completing 50 combat missions.] I'm sure in with a swell bunch of Guys. I sure will be able to save money while I'm over here. There isn't anything to spend it on, so the only thing you can do is save it.

In his letter dated February 19, 1944 he said:

Received your V-Mail letter of the 29th several days ago. I went into a town that's close by and boy what a place. The only place you can go is to the American Red Cross Service Center which is really pretty nice. I've received all your mail OK, even those letters that were sent to Muroc.

A week later, Wanda wrote a letter, dated February 26, 1944 and gave Hazel more details:

Well, I'll get down to points of real interest. I got six letters from George today. I had not heard from him for a month. He is now in Italy. They live in tents and it is chilly. He said the artillery fire could be heard like thunder in the distance. They named their plane "Purple Shaft." The co-pilot bet George they would be home by August. I sure do hope he is right. Perhaps George has written you all this, but I'll take a chance on duplicating. He said he was working on his fox-hole. He also was on a detail to fill rocks around the mess tent — too much mud. I rather think he could be in actual combat by now. I'm keeping my prayers said anyway. He said they had good food. I know he is warm enough because his flying suits are well made and he has two army blankets that are 100% wool.

George's next letter, written on March 6, 1944 is an example of V-Mail:

I'm in town today and am having the name of my plane painted on my jacket. The name of the plane is "The Purple Shaft." What it means can't be explained in a letter so I won't try. I am spending my time in the Red Cross Service Club. It's pretty nice here. I went to the show this afternoon and saw "Aerial Gunner." I've seen it before, but there is nothing else to do so I saw it again. I hope you can read this by the time it's reprinted. *(Fig. 33)*

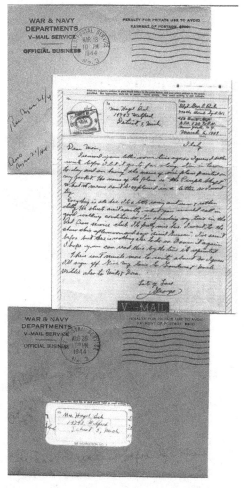

Figure 33: Examples of "V Mail" which was microfilmed, then reprinted at the final destination

Wanda wrote on March 15, 1944 about the challenges of the mail service:

> I'm so glad you've heard from George. My last letter of February 10 was censored. Several lines just cut out! Maybe he tried to say something about a raid. Today I mailed him six packages. Anything under 8 oz. goes thru without a request. So I try to send a few little things. So far he hasn't received any packages. But I'm still hoping for the best. So many of the ships are sunk and mail is lost. But I'm willing to risk it.

George's next short note was written on March 23, 1944 and he said:

> We have been pretty busy the past few days. The only thing wrong with these missions is the flak. *(Fig. 34)*

Figure 34: Explosions of flak during a bombing mission

But outside of that, it isn't bad. Well, Mom, I've got
to take a bath in our little tub (½ a 5 gal. can) so I'll
close for now.

In his next note written on April 20, 1944, a section of
several lines was cut out, similar to Wanda's letter a month
earlier. *(Fig. 35)*

More than a month had passed when Wanda wrote her next
letter on May 5, 1944:

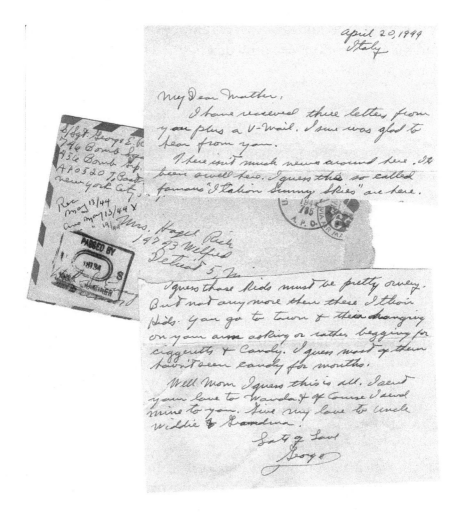

Figure 35: Censored mail with a segment missing from the letter

Mrs. Goodall, the co-pilot's mother sent me this clipping out of the Scranton paper. A few of George's letters have been censored. I wonder if he tried to tell about this flight. When you are thru with the snap and the clipping, I would like to have it back. Mrs. Goodall seems certain that they can all be home this August. I won't mind how long it takes just so they get thru all right.

The newspaper clipping that Wanda sent to Hazel was titled "Lt. Wilson Goodall Relates Vivid Story of Bombing Flight" and the information was provided by the Fifteenth Army Air Force: *(Fig. 36)*

"We have 10 men and a lady in our crew," said Second Lt. Wilson Goodall, copilot of the big B-24 bomber, "Purple Shaft." "The gal was lady luck and she sure was traveling with us that day!" The "Purple Shaft" was on a 15th A.A.F. raid on Nazi airfields at Maniago, Italy, and was just completing its bomb run when a 20 mm. shell from an attacking LE109 pierced its bomb bay.

"What we didn't know at the time," Goodall went on to say, "was that one of our bombs hadn't been released. If the Nazi shell had hit the bomb, we would have had all that high explosive go off in our laps! Fortunately, the Jerry shell hit below the last bomb station, missing the bomb, but jamming the bomb bay mechanism.

When the bomb run had been completed and the Nazi fighters driven off, the "Purple Shaft" started its homeward run. The incendiary bomb cluster worked itself loose and fell on the right bomb bay

SCRANTON FLIER—Lt. Wilson Goodall, 621 North Main Ave., copilot on "Purple Shaft," B-24 bomber, standing on extreme left, has narrow escape on bombing mission over Nazi land.

* * * * *

Lt. Wilson Goodall Relates Vivid Story of Bombing Flight

WEST SCRANTON

FIFTEENTH ARMY AIR FORCE.—"We have 10 men and a lady in our crew," said Second Lt. Wilson Goodall, 24, 621 North Main Ave., Scranton, Pa., copilot of the big B-24 bomber, "Purple Shaft." "The gal was lady luck, and she sure was traveling with us that day!"

The "Purple Shaft" was on a 15th A. A. F. raid on Nazi airfields at Maniago, Italy, and was just completing its bomb run when a 20 mm. shell from a attacking LE109 pierced its bomb bay.

"What we didn't know at the time," Goodall went on, "was that one of our bombs hadn't been released. If the Nazi shell had hit the bomb, we would have had all that high explosive go off in our laps! Fortunately, the Jerry shell hit below the last bomb station, missing the bomb, but jamming the bomb bay mechanism."

When the bomb run had been completed and the Nazi fighters driven off, the "Purple Shaft" started on its homeward run. The incendiary bomb cluster worked itself loose and fell on the right bomb bay door. Due to being jammed, the door only partly opened. Ball turret gunner, Staff Sgt. Russell W. Brown, 21, 1292 Oakwood Ave., Columbus, Ohio, called over the interphone that the bomb bay door was partly open.

Rushing to the bomb bay, the crew knocked out the bomb bay door and let the bomb fall harmlessly into the sea below.

"Lots of freshly cooked fish in the sea that afternoon!" Lieutenant Goodwall said. "That bomb threw up a lot of water...and it almost threw us!"

Figure 36: Article and photograph of the *Purple Shaft* crew taken after a dangerous mission 1944

door. Due to being jammed, the door only partly opened. Ball turret gunner, S/Sgt. Russell Brown, 21, called over the interphone that the bomb bay door was partly open.

Rushing to the bomb bay, the crew knocked out the bomb bay door and let the bomb fall harmlessly into the sea below. "Lots of freshly cooked fish in the sea that afternoon!" Lieutenant Goodall said. "That bomb threw up a lot of water…and it almost threw us!"

Wanda ended her letter by saying:

The Red Cross serves sandwiches and milk to the soldiers on the trains that stop here. I am working with five other girls. We really enjoy doing it.

Both George and Wanda wrote letters on the same day, May 23, 1944. George shared news that a new enlisted men's club had been built on the base. He also told about going up to Naples for two days.

Wanda's letter of May 23rd began:

Well, it's just been one year since George and I were married. It hardly seems like one month. George's father sent me a Lancaster paper with the same write up as the one I sent you. George said he had 23 missions in now. However, they aren't flying as much as they were. George said he had been to Naples. George wired me red roses for my anniversary.

Wanda's next letter, dated May 25, 1944 gave more details about George going to Naples:

Just had a letter from Dale Shields. Her husband is a gunner. She says the co-pilot, Goodall was hit by an ambulance as he stepped out of the plane. He is in the hospital all bruised up. I guess this is holding up the crew so they won't fly until he is up again. I sure hope it isn't serious. No doubt George and the crew went to see him if he is in Naples. I've wondered if George could write me when they have an accident. This apparently was not military, so it came through.

Four days before George's next letter, the Allied Invasion of northern France, known as D-Day, had occurred on June 6, 1944. George was not involved because he and his crew were at a United States Military rest camp on the Isle of Capri. They toured some of the Roman ruins and had a boatman row them inside the Blue Grotto Sea Cave. George said they would go up on the square in the evenings and drink orange juice because drinks cost too much. A Tom Collins or Whiskey Sour cost 50 cents at the bar or 65 cents outside at the tables.

George's letter of June 23, 1944 said:

Wanda is up in N. H. She wanted to go up there and stay until I get back. Boy I wish I could get back there in a hurry and see her. I hope this war & our missions don't last much longer because I don't think my nerves will. I've lost quite a bit of weight which isn't so good for me.

On June 28, 1944 he wrote:

When I confine myself to close shaves, I mean that. It seems I'm always having them. However I'm still alive & running around, altho confined to a hospital. Everything is OK, so don't worry. I'm sorry the news of the invasion upset you so. I imagine a lot of people are upset thinking of their sons in it. I had just got back from Capri when we heard the news. It sure sounded good & of course it sounds better every day. I guess we're staying in the same place. I don't believe we will move up any further. I sure would like to get a glance at Rome, tho. Wanda is up in Lancaster as you no doubt know by now. She decided to go up there & wait until I get back. Boy I sure will be glad to get back to her. I really miss her a lot.

Once again, Hazel had to get more details from Wanda. The letter Wanda wrote on July 16, 1944 had a Manchester, New Hampshire return address:

I have your month old letter here to answer. I should have written sooner, only a lot has happened. As you see by my address, I am in Manchester. I have a four room cottage which is an annex to a large house. I'm working as a clerk in the sportswear department of a store here. George is very pleased to have a place of our own to come back to. George's plane was shot-up over Munich on June 13. George got some flak in one leg. He was released from the hospital on July 5. It couldn't be too serious as he is going to fly again. He now has his first oak leaf cluster to add to his Air Medal, also the Purple Heart. Perhaps George has already written you all this, but I'm not sure. He was psycho-neurotic over this accident at first. But he has had a chance to rest and relax a little. So he's all set to fly, now. I can't see how he can have any more bad luck after all this. I almost wish he wasn't flying anymore but that's his job and he'll have to stick it out. Above all, he certainly isn't yellow. I'm working hard to save all the money I can. Sometimes I feel like a miser but we never know what the future holds.

George wrote again on July 26, 1944 about his injury:

Received your letter of the 13th and was glad to hear from you. I'm sorry you worried about me. There was nothing really wrong with me. I was hurt due to enemy action. I got a piece of flak in the leg. However, it wasn't serious. Also I'm out of the hospital so don't worry any more please.

On August 4, 1944 he wrote:

Everything is OK here. I have forty missions in and only have ten to go. I think I'll be able to make it this month & be home in Sept. I certainly hope so. That little poem you sent sure speaks the truth. The Germans have always been like that I guess. But I don't believe it will happen again. Of course, the Bible says that there will be wars until the coming of the "Prince of Peace." I hope and pray to God that there aren't. It's so senseless. All the killing & ruining of towns & villages & cities. Anyhow if there are wars in the future I hope all my kids are girls. But then they even have a hand in things now. Maybe I shouldn't even bother with any. Everyday I think of the people back home, of the mothers and fathers who get a dreaded telegram. It frightens me a heck of a lot & I hope that you never get one.

Tragically, the next 2 letters in the Black Suitcase, dated August 11 and August 25, 1944, were stamped: MISSING — RETURN TO SENDER. *(Fig. 37)*

On September 6, 1944 Wanda mailed a letter to Hazel about George being reported as missing:

Figure 37: Letters written by Hazel to George which were stamped "Missing, Return to Sender" August 1944

Dear Mother Rich, There are two unanswered letters before me. I've simply been waiting to tell you when George would be home. Yesterday I received a telegram from the government. It stated that George has been reported missing in action since August 22nd over Germany. My last letter was dated Aug 21. He had finished 49 missions then. Well, I've contacted the Red Cross but they can't trace him until I receive a second notice. There is only one thing to do and that is just wait. It was so near the end, I hadn't thought about any more trouble. Some say the European war is nearly over. If George is prisoner of war, it won't be long until he will be back. All we can do is hope and pray for the best. As soon as I get any further word I'll let you know. Perhaps I should have wired you, but I wanted to write to you about it instead. Please don't worry too much. Everything will just have to turn out all right for us. I would write more, but I just can't tonight.

Wanda's next letter was written on September 11, 1944:

Received your lovely surprise box and card. Everything looks so good, but I shall keep it until George comes back. I also received a letter from the Adjutant General. What he has is a "Missing Air Crew Report". However, the case is not closed. If at the end of three months they have no word, he will again write to me. I even felt a little relieved after reading this.

Naturally my parents want me to come home. But I think I'll continue to work here in Manchester to save a little. George still may be coming home soon and this would be our "first home". I'm sure George would want it this way.

I only wish I could write you a more cheerful letter than these last ones. But there is a lot of hope yet and I feel that we should think only that George is safe. It will be a long suspense before we hear from him again, perhaps. But it's worth it to know he is still alive. Fliers really have the best chance of turning up. I feel confident that God will hear our earnest and sincere prayers. George always believed in prayers and he prayed on every mission as he often wrote about it to me. Tomorrow George will be 23 years old. I'm sure he will come back to us and get a chance to live his life from where he left off. He is too young to die. We must be courageous and just wait.

Two weeks later, Wanda wrote on September 28, 1944:

There has been no further word from George but I have heard about two of the crew. The navigator, Robert Thompson, Housatonic, Mass. is dead of wounds received August 22nd. This was reported by the German Gov't to the International Red Cross. Litcher, the tail-gunner, was badly burned on arms and face and has a fractured ankle. The plane is said to have been shot down over Germany. Goodall, the pilot, has not been found. We don't know the names of the rest of the crew. It looks as though they separated while parachuting down. It would seem that if the others were killed or wounded, it would have been reported at the same time. Now, we still have to wait and wait some more. In a way, it is a relief to hear. We know they did have a chance to bail out. If George is a prisoner, it will surely delay his being sent to the South Pacific area. I shall keep writing to you as each bit of news arrives. It may be a long time until I hear again. All we can do is keep on praying and hoping for the best.

On October 18, 1944 Wanda reported:

Just had a letter from the War Dep't. They stated that nine parachutes were seen from George's plane. So they bailed out. The other families all feel that Thompson, the navigator, was killed instantly and didn't bail out. It sounds reasonable. If the pilot was the last to bail out and didn't make it, he would have been reported killed about the same time Thompson was. I feel certain that the boys are alive somewhere.

Douglas Richards the original pilot is now the Squadron Leader. He wrote to his parents this information. He was leading this mission on Aug. 22nd over a place just west of Krakow. Inside the Czech border where the corner of Germany and Poland meet. It was 12 o'clock noon when they hit the target. Capt. Hyde was the co-pilot on Wilson's [Goodall's] plane. He had been with him some time. The names and addresses of all the crew are still being held secret. I got 23 letters back that I wrote to George. Shields, the top gunner, mailed me a box of George's souvenirs. His clothes, etc. come later through the Government. Shields sent his purple heart and campaign ribbons, his New Testament, souvenir money, handkerchiefs and a small jewel box from Capri. The Air Medal wasn't with these things so I don't think George went to headquarters to get it. I'm glad to have these few things as I know George wouldn't want them to get lost.

The next item in the Black Suitcase is a postcard dated November 25, 1944. Wanda wrote:

I am on my way back to W. Va. Somehow I thought the time would go faster if I were at home and could be a little more relaxed. I shall write you a letter after I get home. It's the old address on 9 ½ St., Parkersburg.

On December 26, 1944 Wanda wrote:

We opened our packages on Christmas Eve. Somehow this one was sadder than last year. But there isn't much to be done about it.

The Gov't sent me another letter today. They still have no further word about George or the crew. I did have a letter from Shields. He is one of the gunners who returned to the States in Sept. He wrote that since George was wounded last June, he just wasn't the jolly fellow who went over with them. He was entirely too serious. I'm afraid George has changed and will be even more changed since this last accident. But I don't blame George — it isn't weakness on his part. This War will be blamed for many things.

Wanda wrote her next letter on January 7, 1945:

I'm glad you liked the bed jacket. You've kept me in touch with yourself so well and we haven't even seen each other yet. I always look forward to getting a letter from you. I feel as though I've known you all my life.

Howard Shields wrote me an interesting letter a few days ago. He is at Keesler Field, Miss. He is talking about the Munich raid on June 13. "George was wounded the same day as the engineer [Krenek] was hurt so bad. It was in one leg, the right one, I believe. A piece of flak hit about eight inches below the knee on the fore part of his leg. It was not a bad wound but his Doctor tried to heal it up too soon. It healed on the outside and not in the center so had to be reopened, and then healed up slowly. The scar was not very large and no limp. Luckily, it did not hit the bone. I remember we kidded him so much about it. He had taken a fall from the motorcycle the day before and had some scratches on his legs. We told him he was just working for a purple heart. It was really nothing to kid about, but that was all in the crew, you know. He did not want to fly after that and the rest of us were saying the same thing, but it was fly or else. There wasn't a boy on the crew that would back out."

Then he told me the government should send the Air Medal to me. It has four oak leaf clusters. Also his clothes, but all this takes time and red tape, I reckon. I knew you'd like to know all this, so I copied it word for word. This is probably all the information I'll ever get until George comes back. Shields was closer to him than most of the other boys. They were the only married men on the plane. Perhaps that could be one of the reasons.

Tuesday I have an appointment to take a Civil Service exam. So I may have a job soon. One of the

Doctors would like for me to be his receptionist. But we haven't come to terms on the hours and pay, yet. The family have gone to him for several years. He is a grand person and I hate to refuse. But maybe we can settle it some way.

In her February 4, 1945 letter Wanda reported:

Capt. Hyde, the co-pilot on George's plane is now a prisoner of Germany. They are slow at turning up, but the silence is beginning to break. Surely with all the new gains we'll hear from the other boys soon.

Finally took my Civil Exam but haven't heard the results yet. There is a Government Hospital at White Sulphur Springs. I have seriously thought of going over and applying for a job. Most openings would be thru Civil Service so I'll have to wait for my rating before I look into it. Then, sometimes I think it would be better to wait until I hear from George. But I sure do feel useless just staying at home doing nothing at a time like this.

Sometime during the next 12 days, Wanda evidently made contact with Hazel because in her February 16, 1945 letter Wanda expressed the sadness of George's death.

(*Fig. 38*) Dear Mother Rich, Yours was the first letter I received and it helped so much. Today I had a letter from the War Dep't. They have no details or information on George's death. The German Gov't reported thru the International Red Cross. Simply he died on Aug. 22, 1944. Mrs. Colletti, also got a wire on Feb. 12 that her son 1st Lt. Nicholas C. was killed on Aug. 22. Just received a card from Mrs. Babcock. Her son

Frank is reported killed on the same day. It certainly looks bad now. Counting Thompson and George, it makes four killed on the same day. Hyde and Litcher are prisoners. Four men are still unaccounted. It is still so vague I just can't believe that George is gone. These reports are carefully checked so it must be final. It is even harder to believe after waiting these six long months. Will we ever know what did actually happen? These days are hard ones to live. I had to quit my job but keep busy with just letter writing. It's the one thing no one else can do for me. I will write you more the next time. Just wanted you to know the latest on the boys and that I was thinking of you. I know your sorrow is as great as mine. There

Figure 38: Sympathy cards received by Hazel February 1945

isn't much I can say to console you now, but my sincerest sympathy is all yours. Lovingly, Wanda

Wanda's next letter was written on March 7, 1945:

Received your letter a few days ago. I must say you expressed your feelings in the same way I do. I don't believe I shall ever think of George as dead until after the War. Somehow, I get a hunch he is around over there in hiding. When Litcher comes home and explains that raid to me in person I'll be convinced. But I'm not giving up hope until then. I understand that Litcher has Thompson's ring. He must have jumped with Litcher and Hyde, then died in the hospital.

This picture was taken after the June 13th raid. That was when George got flak in his leg. Here is the story as Mrs. Richards wrote it to me.

"I don't know what to say to comfort you, but I want you to know that your husband was a real hero and should have a special citation. I may be repeating what you already know, if so please excuse me, but I want you to know that he really saved two lives by his courage and cool headedness. It was when the anti-aircraft bomb went right through the plane and exploded on the opposite side. I'm enclosing a picture in case you haven't one. *(Fig. 39)* Krenek, the engineer was hanging out the hole with one hand and with both ankles shattered. Brown was thrown up several feet and his oxygen mask knocked off. Your husband pulled Krenek in and gave first-aid, got Brown fixed up with oxygen before any of the other crew could leave their posts. I think your

Figure 39: Damage to the underbelly of the *Purple Shaft* acquired during a bombing raid over Munich, Germany June 13, 1944

husband was injured also. Nichol [Nickel] told us all of this. He said Douglas tried to get a medal for George but it was turned down. Which irked the crew very much because some get medals for only spectacular things but this was really saving lives."

Well, Mother Rich, our George was a great hero even if he didn't get a medal for it. You are the only one I've told this to. I had not intended to mention it but I feel so bad about it I'll just have to. George's father has never written me one word since I left New Hamp. in November. I wrote to him twice and also wired him. I was made to feel as though I wasn't good enough for George. So that ends that. I would like to tell Guy these things about George. But he has made it quite clear he does not want any thing further to do with me. I am terribly ashamed that he has taken this attitude, but there is not a thing I can do about it. I have always been nice to Guy and I have tried to understand him. But since I have failed, all I can do is put it behind me and keep going. I know very little about his private life. George knew even less than that.

Even tho I have not actually met you in person, I feel very close to you. There will be many things to talk over when we do meet. I hope it will be in the near future.

Two weeks later, on March 21, 1945 Wanda wrote:

Received your last letter and I was very happy to get it. Tell Uncle Widdie I sure appreciated his warm welcome.

First of all, I want to tell you about George's Insurance. His father is to collect it and if any thing happens to him, it goes to you, because George named you as contingent. This is the way it was made out before we were married and that is how it stands. In my estimation, it throws even a poorer light on Guy's character because now a lot of things take on a new meaning. For instance, when George was reported missing, Guy said he'd never work another day. Guess he knew what the future held. George always knew I only married him because I loved him. That was the only item I had in mind or ever shall have. I loved George very deeply and I shall always be in love with the memory of him. If Guy chooses to think otherwise, it won't matter because his opinions don't count in my estimation.

As far as I know, I won't be working for a while. My applications haven't been answered yet. I even tried for Washington, D. C. but they had all the Civil Service workers they needed. So I'm still on the shelf. I'm still planning to visit you this summer. I noticed the snaps in George's album of the zoo. It looks very interesting.

Wanda's next letter was written a month later, on April 22, 1945 with a postmark from Huntington, West Virginia. She told about her new job:

My Civil Service appointment finally came thru. I am a naval inspector of war materials for the Sylvania Electric Products Co. here in Huntington. There are ten of us with a supervisor. Lt. Riedell of the Navy is our chief. We have separate hours from the factory workers. Eight A.M to 4:45 P.M. We are not responsible to anyone at Sylvania and we have the Navy behind us in any decisions we make. This work is a complete change from any thing I've done before and I really enjoy doing it. The plant has a grand cafeteria where we get our breakfast and lunch.

Every other Saturday I have off. As it is only four hours on the bus to Parkersburg, I can easily go home. I got a nice sleeping room in a private home thru the Y.W.C.A. So now I'm fairly well settled.

We are allowed sick leave and annual leave so I can easily arrange a trip to Detroit this summer. Some how, I feel a little more helpful to the War effort since I'm in the swing of things again.

Here I am rattling on about myself. Things are looking better in Europe these days. As the armies are well up in Czhech [*sic*], I keep wondering if some of the crew might turn up. It's a distant hope and not very sensible I guess but it doesn't ever hurt to keep on hoping.

The next letter in the Black Suitcase was written on May 31, 1945 and Wanda wrote more about visiting Detroit:

As far as I know I can come to Detroit around the first week in August. I have been asked to go to Marietta, O. to do the same kind of work. This is a new plant twelve miles from Parkersburg. So I'll stay at home again. Anyway I'll probably be here in Huntington for most of the summer. I'll let you know the exact dates of my vacation when it is settled.

So far I haven't heard a word about the two boys who were POW's. There must be a lot of confusion over there and all these cases take a lot of time to get straightened out.

With the price of clothes so high and the quality so low, I'm trying to make a few dresses of my own. Mother is making a stripped chambray and I'm working on a border print. What little bit I sew in the evening does not make much head-way. But eventually I'll finish.

Wanda's next letter was written on July 15, 1945 from Parkersburg, West Virginia:

Received your letter some time ago, but have been waiting for some definite plans to tell you.

Have been sent to the Marietta plant for two weeks, July 16th to 28th. The inspector there is on her vacation. Then my vacation starts on July 30 to Aug 4. After I find out the exact times and means of travel I will wire you when I am to arrive in Detroit. This is more like a three week vacation instead of one week. I am staying at home and going to work by street car.

We have an old camera and no film. The number is A116. I'll bring it along just in case we could get some film.

The Gov't sent me a notice that George is to be awarded posthumously the Silver Star and the Air Medal with four Oak Leaf clusters. The Silver Star is for his actions last June 13th when he was first wounded. I believe I wrote you in detail of how he saved Krenek's life. I'll bring a few letters you will probably like to read. The two P.O.W boys are at home now. But they have nothing further to add to what the Gov't has already said.

I'm looking forward to meeting all of you.

Wanda's trip to Detroit had ended when she wrote her next letter dated Monday August 6, 1945 from Huntington, West Virginia. [On this same day, the American B-29 bomber Enola Gay dropped the world's first atom bomb over the city of Hiroshima, Japan.] Wanda wrote:

Arrived right on schedule all the way down the line. I even got to work on time this morning.

My vacation was absolutely perfect. I enjoyed every minute of it. I just knew you and Uncle Bill [George's "Uncle Widdie"] and Grandma would be just as grand as you were. I kept wishing George could have been with us, too.

Our lives continue to go on, but his had to end so abruptly — that's what makes me so bitter about the whole thing. He was just beginning to live. I really don't mind for my own selfish reasons. I'm just thankful that fate was good enough to let me share his life. George was so good and kind that he made me better in my ways of thinking.

This may not make sense at all but I'm sure you can understand what I'm trying to say.

My transfer to the Marietta plant is for next Monday. [Which would have been August 13. The next day, August 14, 1945 it was announced that Japan had surrendered unconditionally to the Allies, effectively ending World War II. Since then both August 14 and August 15 have been known as "Victory over Japan Day."] The girl who is there has asked to come back to Huntington as she is too lonesome. Well, I'm glad to go, but I don't like the idea of having to shoulder all the responsibility. But the Lt. has assured me he isn't worried so I guess I shouldn't be either. Now I'll have another move to make this week-end.

Give my regards to those I met. Don't forget to fill out your blank from the Gov't. I feel you deserve every bit of it.

Wanda was still in Huntington when she wrote her next letter on August 27, 1945. She told about her new job:

> Received your nice long letter, the beautiful hose, the pictures and the camera. Thanks a lot for everything.
>
> As you can see, I'm still here. I was all packed to go to Marietta when the War news broke. So my orders were cancelled. We worked right along thru the 18th and then four of us were transferred to the Vet Hosp. here. So now I'm a file clerk in the mail and records office for the Army. Guess we were pretty lucky to have such a nice boss.
>
> The snap shots are very good, I think. Especially that informal pose of you and me on Belle Isle. *(Fig. 40)*
>
> Has Uncle Bill's job been affected by any cut back? I had the impression that the plant could easily convert to peace time work. The war won't really seem over

Figure 40: Hazel Elliott Rich and Wanda Bee Rich, Belle Isle, Michigan August 1945

until all the boys are home again. The celebrating was quite mild here.

I'm not any too pleased with my new job. With the Navy Dep't I sat all day and now I'm on my feet all day. Wouldn't it be nice if I could hit a happy medium? Nearly everyone was thrown out of work in all these small towns so I guess I'm better off than most girls. However, if I can find some thing I like better I'll make the change in a hurry.

I want you to know that I'd feel perfectly at home to drop in at your house just any time, Mother Rich and I hope you will feel the same towards me. My folks would enjoy knowing you very much.

In her next letter, dated September 5, 1945 Wanda said:

Everything is quite upset at the Vet's Administration. There are so many transfers and so many new cases. I have almost decided to give up my job entirely. There is a very good college here and I am thinking of enrolling. I've been told that you are never too old to learn. This isn't such a bad little town if I was busy studying I wouldn't notice it very much, either.

The following month, on October 18, 1945 Wanda wrote about college:

I resigned from Civil Serv. and enrolled at Marshall College here in Hunt [Huntington]. It is chiefly a teachers' college. My major is Home Economics. It really isn't as bad as I expected. I doubt if I can get my degree, I'll probably end up sewing slip-covers again. My subjects are Eng. Literature, Social Studies,

Textiles & Fabrics, Applied Art, and Nutrition. They are all very interesting. It is a little hard to study after being out for five years.

Have your papers carried a description of the radio proximity fuse made for the Navy? Well, that is the little item we inspected here. Our Lt. Comdr. was in charge of six of the plants. It is an interesting little gadget — and many were seen in my sleep — Ha!

The Vet's Administration here is being transferred to Charleston, W. Va. However, your case may be taken care of before they move.

The snap-shots you've sent me are a nice remembrance. I get them out occasionally and think of the grand week I spent in your home. *(Fig. 41 – 42)*

On December 7, 1945 Wanda wrote:

Well, since I'm better acquainted at school, several people have suggested to me to go into Social work. They must take me for a "hoo – dinny." I can't learn everything at once. So I'll just keep plugging as I am and trust to fate for a solution as to a career. Don and Lee are no doubt enjoying civilian life to the upmost [*sic*]. How does Don like school?

The last letter in the Black Suitcase was dated January 29, 1946. *(Fig. 43)* In it, Wanda wrote:

Finally did receive a letter from the Gov't since the capture of Germany's records. The plane crashed in the vicinity of Wiel, Germany. George and the other boys were buried on Aug. 24, 1944 in the cemetery

Figure 41: Wanda and Hazel, Detroit, Michigan August 1945

Figure 42: Willard C. Elliott, George's "Uncle Widdie," and Wanda, Detroit August 1945

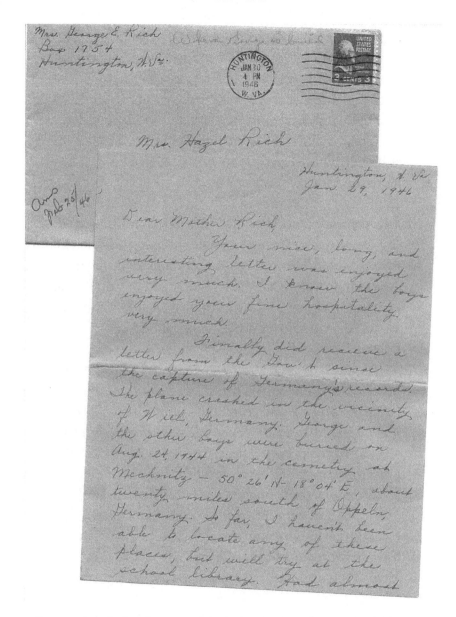

Figure 43: The last letter in the Black Suitcase, written by Wanda January 29, 1946

at Mechnitz — 50° 26' N - 18° 04' E about twenty miles south of Oppeln, Germany. So far, I haven't been able to locate any of these places, but will try at the school library. Had almost given up hope of ever hearing anything further about the accident. Perhaps you've already gotten this information. Am still waiting for the time to come when I'll see it has happened for the best.

The second semester starts in the morning. Am all registered under Home Ec. major, so guess I'll stick by it. Will be a junior in Sept. which doesn't seem so far away. Here are my New classes: Social Studies, Home Decoration, Elem. Sewing, English, Child Care and Phys. Ed. I think they are all very interesting.

Really had a streak of luck last week. I found a two room apartment across the street from the Campus. Just a bedroom and kitchen, but it already seems like home. I brought a few odds and ends down this week-end from Parkersburg. As soon as I make the kitchen curtains, I'll be all settled. There is an electric refrigerator, four burner gas stove with built-in oven, kitchen cabinet, table, chairs and sink — also my own desk is in the kitchen. The bedroom has a four-poster double bed, large dresser, rocker and a wool rug and pad.

Have my own front entrance and a back porch from the kitchen with stairs to the yard. You may think that is all the good features, but the rent is only $7.00 per week. There is quite a bad housing problem here, so I think I'm very fortunate. In Textiles class, I wove a rug of four-ply cotton yarn. This is the center of attraction on the kitchen floor.

It is very probable that Wanda and Hazel continued their correspondence during the subsequent years. However, the contents of the Black Suitcase end with the January 1946 letter written by Wanda. The Black Suitcase is truly a time-capsule of George Elliott Rich's life from his birth in 1921 to his death in 1944. *(Fig. 44)* It is also a treasure chest not only of original family documents, but an insight into the life and times of average Americans during the Great Depression and World War II.

The uniqueness of the Black Suitcase as a treasure chest will become evident when the reader delves into the next section: "Fifth Graders Focus on the Forties." Interwoven with the fifth graders' discoveries will be a section called "Where's Wanda?" The events that occurred during 1991-1995 will be shared in chronological order. There are a number of coincidences, in what the students called "The Black Suitcase Mystery," that will be noted when they occur in the narrative.

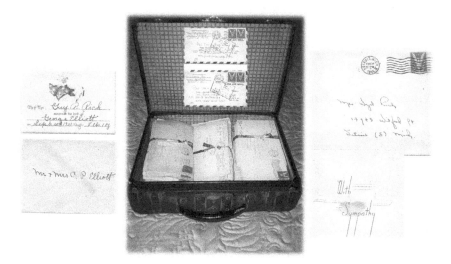

Figure 44: The Black Suitcase: a time capsule of George Elliott Rich's life

1991-1995
FIFTH GRADERS
FOCUS
ON THE FORTIES

WELCOME!

BLACK SUITCASE

World War II
Night

MARK TWAIN SCHOOL

DECEMBER 6, 1991

BY Eric Langworth

W.W.II

Fifth Graders Focus on the Forties

During the four years, 1991-1995, of the World War II project, Mark Twain Elementary School did not have much in the way of modern technology. The one fax machine in the district was located in the central administration building, the library had one Apple IIE computer that used five-inch floppy disks to display programs, and Internet connections did not exist. All correspondence and long-distance research was done the "old fashioned" way by writing letters.

The reader is reminded that in 1991, Gail Elliott (Thomas) Downs, the current guardian of the Black Suitcase, was the Elementary School Librarian for the Brentwood School District, near St. Louis, Missouri. A fifth-grade teacher had asked if Gail had anything in the library that might get the students interested in genealogy. Gail suggested the students might learn the basics of genealogy by reading the family documents stored in the suitcase. The activities were planned as supplemental library sessions and were scheduled for the last two weeks in May. *(Fig. 1)*

Figure 1: Librarian Gail Elliott Thomas presenting the Black Suitcase to fifth-grade students

The "Black Suitcase Mystery" might have ended with the 1946 letter in the small suitcase, except for the newspaper clipping from Lockport, New York. Lockport was the home town of Doug Richards, the pilot of the *Purple Shaft*. Wanda received two copies of the clipping, so she had mailed one to Hazel. According to the caption, Dan Curran, the other person pictured, was from St. Louis, Missouri. The article reads:

> *Union-Sun & Journal*, Lockport, NY, Wednesday, July 12, 1944: LUCKY ESCAPE — 1ˢᵗ Lieut. Douglas C. Richards, pilot of the B-24 Liberator bomber, the *Purple Shaft*, smiles "it's lucky this hole wasn't someplace else or we wouldn't be here to tell about it," as he examines the damage done by German flak during a bombing mission over Germany. His copilot, [newspaper error: Dan was the bombardier, not copilot] Lieut. Daniel F. Curran Jr., of St. Louis, Mo., also breathes a sigh of relief. *(Fig. 2)*

After Gail read the article and discovered the St. Louis coincidence, she checked the local phone book and found a listing for Dan Curran! Gail made contact with the Curran family and learned that Dan had survived the war, but had died in 1986. His widow, Eleanor Curran, stated that their second son was named after pilot Doug Richards and the two families had remained friends since World War II. She wondered if Gail would like to have Doug Richard's address. Eleanor also gave Gail a clipping printed in a 1944 St. Louis newspaper which matched the photo in the New York article, stored for almost 50 years in the Black Suitcase! *(Fig. 3)* The only difference being the St. Louis hero was credited with the quote:

> *St. Louis Globe Democrat*, July 11, 1944: IT'S LUCKY this hole wasn't somewhere else or we wouldn't be here to tell about it," says Lt. Daniel F. Curran, St. Louis, copilot [Newspaper error: Dan was the bombardier, not copilot] of a Liberator in Italy. His pilot, Lt. Douglas C. Richards, Lockport, N.Y., seems happy about the whole thing, too.

Figure 2: Lockport, New York newspaper article kept in the Black Suitcase since 1944

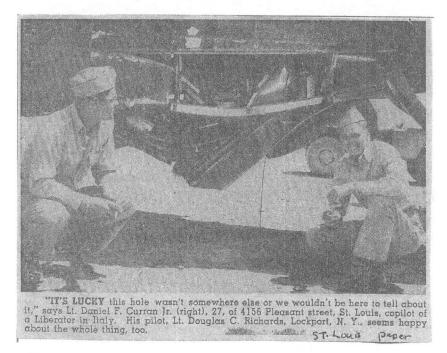

"IT'S LUCKY this hole wasn't somewhere else or we wouldn't be here to tell about it," says Lt. Daniel F. Curran Jr. (right), 27, of 4156 Pleasant street, St. Louis, copilot of a Liberator in Italy. His pilot, Lt. Douglas C. Richards, Lockport, N. Y., seems happy about the whole thing, too. ST. Louis paper

Figure 3: Saint Louis, Missouri newspaper clipping given to Gail May 1991

Gail was excited about the St. Louis connection to the story. As planned with their teacher, the Black Suitcase was opened and presented to the fifth graders for the first time on Monday, May 20, 1991. They were surprised to see the two 1944 newspaper clippings, with identical photographs, that had been published in different parts of the country. When they were told that Gail knew how to contact the pilot of the *Purple Shaft* they immediately started listing their questions. With their help, Gail wrote a letter, dated May 23rd, to Doug Richards and explained the contents of the Black Suitcase. She told him about the fifth graders' interest and asked for more information about George Elliott Rich:

> Dear Doug,
>
> This letter will probably be a touch with your past. It concerns one of your WWII crew mates on the

Purple Shaft, George Elliott Rich. I met a long-time friend of yours this month, Eleanor Curran (Mrs. Daniel F.) and she suggested I write to you.

Please let me explain who I am: George Elliott Rich, the radio operator on the *Purple Shaft* was my dad's cousin. George's mother, my great-aunt, saved all the correspondence she received from her son. When she died in 1979, my family inherited all George's letters. For almost 50 years, they've been stored in a small, battered suitcase.

I am a teacher/librarian in a St. Louis area school district. I enjoy doing genealogy and have been introducing a group of fifth graders to the hobby. One of the activities I planned involved discovering information about George by reading the old newspaper clippings and letters.

I'm hoping you might be able to tell me when/where George was killed. His mother had reports that he was "missing in action" in August, 1944. I couldn't find any official death notice, but did find sympathy cards sent by friends and family.

Eleanor Curran thought she remembered hearing Dan say, "Wilson Goodall, Robert Thompson and Rich" were killed together. Is that true? Did the *Purple Shaft* get hit or were they on a different plane?

In the Nov. 1990 Vol. III #4 "456 Bomb Group" newsletter, I read where someone had sent in a memorial in honor of Goodall: "He (Goodall) was flying the *Purple Shaft* on his 50th mission over

Blechammer [*sic*], Germany (Aug. '44) when they got a direct hit." Do you know —was George Rich on the same plane? My fifth graders and I would certainly like to know what happened. Eleanor told me that after 50 missions, crew members could rotate back to the states. Was this true? Is that why you and Dan were not with the others?

We'd also like to know more about the 746th Bomb Squadron. Where were you stationed? Eleanor mentioned Italy — were you also in England? Did you have one particular area of Germany that the 746th covered? Did the same crew always fly the same plane? Did other crews fly the *Purple Shaft*? What became of the plane? And how did it get its name?

I know I've asked a lot of questions and it will take some time to get your reply. The school year is almost over now, but the classroom teacher is excited about this project. She wants to start earlier next year and expand the unit further.

As you can see, I have a lot of questions. My school kids are really excited about this project and I'm enjoying seeing "history come alive" to them. And isn't this a great tribute to George and the others who were killed? Their memory will live on in the minds of these kids, almost fifty years after the war.

Thanks in advance, Doug, for any help you can give us.

A week later, on May 30, 1991, before school ended for the year, Doug responded with a letter and a 17 page summary of his World War II experiences:

Dear Gail,

I keep finding it is a small world as it relates to WWII. I often have people call who were with me in Italy.

I will try to answer your letter in NC, but my records are with my daughter in Blacksburg, VA. She will forward this letter to you along with my war history which after much prodding she had me write. I have one of the best photo albums of anyone in our Group I have been told.

My eyes become moist when you mentioned Rich's name. George was a good young man. I remember him as a serious, competent radio operator. He was a steadying influence on the rest of the enlisted men.

George was killed Aug. 22, 1944 over Blechammer [*sic*], Germany (now Ujazd, Poland). George and the rest of us came together as a crew at Muroc Lake, California (now Edwards Air Force Base). (Date in my orders 1943). My war history has names of members of crew. We were a crew of 10 young men. There were about 20 crews per squadron. There were 4 squadrons in a Group. We trained in B-24's for about 3 months before leaving Muroc in Dec. 1943 to pick up a brand new airplane for our trip to Italy. This plane became the *Purple Shaft*. It was named by Goodall because he felt we had been shafted by not being in fighter planes (see p. 10 of war history).

We were stationed in the Foggia area of Italy near Stenora and Cerignola. Our bomber group reunion is going back to Foggia in 1993.

We flew all over the Balkans, northern Italy, southern France, Germany, Austria-Hungary empire. Blechammer was in Silesia where coal was used in making synthetic fuel.

The *Purple Shaft* was our airplane and we usually flew it if it was operational. We would fly once or twice a week. The Group would fly 7 days a week if possible.

We flew the *Shaft* to Bad Vaslau, Austria. Rich was in the crew. We were attacked by German fighters on the way to the target. One of our squadron planes was shot down and we were hit with a rocket. Jerry Krenek, our flight engineer and left waist gunner was wounded in his shoulder. We had over 500 holes in the plane from the rocket.

Later on a trip to Munich, we had a direct hit, putting a 4 foot wide hole in the bottom of the plane near where Krenek was standing. His feet were crushed and he spent a year and a half in the hospital. I had the pleasure of being with Krenek in Tucson, Ariz. a month ago at our bomb group reunion. That was the first time I had seen him in all those years.

After that Munich flight, the *Purple Shaft* never flew in combat again. The plane was hit more than any other plane in the squadron.

I believe my history relates Blechammer as I remember. The three men who were killed were on their last mission. Captain Hyde, the Operations Officer of the 746th, was flying as copilot and deputy command pilot. Goody was 1st pilot. I was flying as command pilot so they were on my right wing 50-100' away when they were blown up. I didn't know Capt. Hyde was alive until 4 years ago. I also had the pleasure of spending 4 days with him and his wife in Tucson at our bomb group reunion. He was West Point and stayed in the service, getting out a Colonel. I will suggest to him that he write his account of Blechammer and possibly his prison camp experiences. I will send him a copy of your letter.

I believe my history covers what I have missed in letter. I will send copies of photos when I get up to my daughter's place in July.

The reason we didn't finish our missions as a crew was that some of the officers took positions of leading Group from time to time with other crews. We flew most of the time as a crew. On the Blechammer mission, Litcher, tail turret gunner, was from our crew. He was blown out of the airplane when it exploded and his chute was burned open. Thompson was alive when he hit the ground, but he died from loss of blood. Hyde ministered to him as best he could.

I will see what more I can send you this summer.

Sincerely,
Douglas Richards

The last two weeks of May 1991, during the time Gail was corresponding with Doug Richards, the original group of fifth-grade students started reading the contents of the Black Suitcase. They soon discovered the letters dealt with World War II and the Army Air Corps. Just a few months prior to this, the Desert Storm Conflict had occurred, so the boys were immediately intrigued with George's military experiences on the B-24 Liberator. The girls thought George looked like Tom Cruise so they, also, were willing to learn about the contents of the Black Suitcase! *(Fig. 4)*

Figure 4: 1942 Army portrait of George Elliott Rich who resembled the actor Tom Cruise according to the fifth-grade girls in 1991

The Desert Storm Conflict, with events broadcast each day on television, had lasted just a few months. The students soon realized that World War II continued for several years. The first indication that something might have happened to George were two letters, which Hazel mailed in August 1944, that were stamped "Return — Missing in Action." The fifth graders knew that George needed 50 missions before he could return to the States. They were devastated after reading Wanda's September 5, 1944 letter which stated that "George was reported missing on August 22." In that letter, Wanda wrote that her most recent letter from George had been dated August 21 and he said he had completed 49 missions. As Wanda had written, "It was so near the end, I hadn't thought about any more trouble."

Those students, in May, 1991, suddenly realized that if he had just been able to safely finish that 50th mission, George might have had an entire life with Wanda. Hazel might have had grandchildren and the Black Suitcase would have remained merely a storage box for a mother's keepsakes.

School year 1990-1991 ended on a high note for Gail, the fifth-grade students and their teacher. Gail realized that the Black Suitcase offered the students a unique view of World War II and that the 50th Anniversary of Pearl Harbor would occur in just a few months, on December 7th 1991. During the summer, Gail met with Jackie Whitworth, the principal of Mark Twain Elementary School, and fifth-grade teacher Leslie Brann to make plans to commemorate that event. The semester-long World War II study, culminating in Mark Twain Elementary School's "Pearl Harbor Night" on December 6, 1991, became the beginning of a four year project, 1991-1995, which gained national recognition for the school.

It will become evident that the three educators formed a strong team. They were all born during the first year of the Baby Boom Era, their respective parents having met and married during World War II. *(Fig. 5)* The fifth-grade project could not have developed to the extent it did without the support of the

Figure 5: Mark Twain Elementary School educators: Librarian Gail Elliott Thomas, Principal Jackie Whitworth and Fifth Grade Language Arts Teacher Leslie Brann

Brentwood School District Superintendent, Dr. John Cleary. In addition to having a doctorate in School Administration, he was a full colonel in the United States Army Reserves and had been activated in 1991 to support Desert Storm. He gave his approval to the idea of commemorating the 50th Anniversary of Pearl Harbor.

FIRST YEAR OF THE PROJECT:
School Year 1991-1992, First Semester

September - December

In September 1991, the Black Suitcase Mystery was presented to the new class of fifth graders and they began to learn about George Elliott Rich and his bride, Wanda. To offer the students extra experiences, a weekly after-school session called The

Wednesday Club met in the school's library. Members of the Brentwood Historical Society were especially helpful. The president of the society wrote the following in her letter to the membership:

> I have recommended you to join in helping with an exciting project the librarian at Mark Twain School is spearheading. December 7, 1991, marks the 50th anniversary of Pearl Harbor and the beginning of World War II. Through memorabilia, letters and news articles, the students will learn about that period in our country's history and at the same time will learn something about genealogy. From us, hopefully they will learn something about the Homefront during the war. Where were you during the War years? How did your folks at home support our troops? How did it affect your family? What do you remember? Share your memories with the fifth graders. EVERYONE IS needed to make this part of the project successful. Don't say let somebody else do it!!! You're the important one. Bring a friend.

In addition to the local historical society, World War II veterans, retired teachers and local citizens came to Mark Twain School to share their first-hand accounts of life during the war. Students examined books and photographs depicting life in the 1940s while having the help of those who lived during that time. *(Fig. 6)* Some even learned how to knit because school children in the 1940s helped the war effort by knitting squares which were then sewn together to make blankets.

Of particular interest was a World War II veteran who told of his experiences as a radio operator and waist gunner on a B-24 Liberator. *(Fig. 7)* He held the same positions as George Elliott Rich, the hero of the Black Suitcase Mystery.

Figure 6: Fifth-grade students at an after-school session of the weekly Wednesday Club joined by members of the Brentwood Historical Society October 1991

As December approached, the fifth graders made posters to promote the special World War II Night scheduled for Friday, December 6, 1991. The art teacher helped students with their designs and the gym teacher taught them how to jitterbug. During music class, the teacher introduced songs from the 1940s and the students practiced singing "Mairzy Doats," "Praise the Lord and Pass the Ammunition" and "Boogie Woogie Bugle Boy."

Additionally, the fifth graders eagerly anticipated the visit of a very special guest. They had written a letter to Doug Richards on October 8, 1991:

Dear Mr. Richards,

Our library teacher is Mrs. Gail Elliott Thomas and her relative was George Elliott Rich. He flew on the *Purple Shaft* with you in 1944.

Our fifth-grade class is studying World War II. We would like you to come and visit Mark Twain School in Brentwood, Missouri, a suburb of St. Louis. We would like you to tell us about W.W. II. If you do come, please bring your scrapbook and other memorabilia.

We are having a World War II Night at school on December 6th, the night before the 50th anniversary of Pearl Harbor. We will pay for your airfare and refreshments if you are able to come.

Please write us back as soon as possible with your answer.

Your admirers,
The Fifth Graders of Mark Twain School

Figure 7: Guest speaker Ralph Piña, WWII radio operator/waist gunner on a B-24 Liberator Bomber December 4, 1991

With the financial help of the parent group at Mark Twain School, Doug Richards, the pilot of the *Purple Shaft* and George's former commander flew from North Carolina to St. Louis. *(Fig. 8)* The Wednesday Club session on December 4th was truly exciting because a crew from a St. Louis television station filmed the session and broadcast the footage the following day.

Figure 8: Doug Richards, pilot of the *Purple Shaft* being introduced by Gail to students at the Wednesday Club session December 4, 1991

Also during this time period, several local newspapers heard about Mark Twain Elementary School's special World War II project. Articles and pictures were published in the following:

> *The Pulse*, Brentwood, Missouri, November 1991: In Touch With Our Past: Senior Citizens Remembering-Students Discovering

Mid-County Journal, St. Louis, Missouri, November 19, 1991: School Project Brings World War II Alive for Students

St. Louis Post-Dispatch, St. Louis, Missouri, December 6, 1991: Mementos Offer Class a Glimpse of WWII

The Pulse, Brentwood, Missouri, January 1992: WWII Service Men and Women Honored

Doug Richards spent Friday morning, December 6th with the fifth graders, telling them his recollections of George and the missions they flew in the *Purple Shaft*. *(Fig. 9)* He and his wife enjoyed lunch with the students in the school cafeteria. In their "thank you" letters written on December 18, 1991, two students commented about the seating arrangements.

Figure 9: Doug Richards talking to fifth graders Friday morning December 6, 1991

A girl wrote:

> Dear Mr. Richards, I want to thank you for coming
> to Mark Twain. I really want to thank you for bringing
> your wife and eating lunch with the girls and not
> with the boys.

One of the boys wrote:

> Dear Mr. Richards, You were probably the star of
> World War II Night. It was too bad you didn't bring
> any of your medals and decorations. We didn't need
> to see how good you were. All we needed to see was
> your personality. You probably would of had more
> fun eating with the boys instead of the girls.

Doug and his wife departed after lunch, then the students decorated the gym in preparation for the evening's events. It was a huge success! The gym was packed and the audience tapped their toes as the fifth graders danced the jitterbug and sang their songs. The 1940s research projects were well done and displayed attractively.

An unexpected honor occurred when Gail, on behalf of the Mark Twain fifth-grade students and staff, received a Resolution from the Missouri House of Representatives which read, in part:

> WHEREAS, on December 7, 1991, citizens across this
> nation will observe the Fiftieth Anniversary of the
> Japanese attack on Pearl Harbor, a truly monumental
> event which initiated U.S. involvement in World War
> II and changed forever the face of world politics; and

> WHEREAS, this observance will mark the culmina-
> tion of a project undertaken by fifth graders at Mark
> Twain Elementary to relive the history of World

War II by directly examining writings, artifacts, oral accounts, and other materials pertinent to the time period; and

WHEREAS, this most innovative project was initiated by Mark Twain Librarian Gail Elliott Thomas, who was inspired to offer this unique learning opportunity to students by a black suitcase she inherited from her great-aunt which contained a first account of the war through the perspective of George Elliott Rich, a sergeant in the Army Air Corps; and

WHEREAS, Mark Twain Elementary students participating in this project have gained a valuable insight into one of the most monumental events in history by reading the personalized accounts of George Elliott Rich, meeting with members of the Brentwood Historical Society to listen to their stories of the war, collecting and examining World War II items, and taking part in a variety of activities connected to events during the war era; and

WHEREAS, during the upcoming World War II Evening, the Mark Twain fifth graders will have a special opportunity to meet with the pilot of the *Purple Shaft* airplane on which George Elliott Rich served, Mr. Doug Richards:

NOW, THEREFORE, BE IT RESOLVED that we, the members of the Missouri House of Representatives, Eighty-sixth General Assembly, hereby join unanimously in commending and applauding Gail Elliott Thomas and all the students and faculty involved with the project at Mark Twain Elementary School for their admirable efforts in honoring the Fiftieth Anniversary of Pearl Harbor and America's proud record of involvement during the Second World War.

Gail felt truly humbled that the Black Suitcase project received such recognition. George's story, and countless others like it, had a terribly sad ending in 1944. However, almost 50 years later, it was helping students better understand how World War II affected America.

After the program, members of the Brentwood Historical Society, dressed as "Donut Dollies" served refreshments, including SPAM and crackers plus Ovaltine at the "Canteen" in the corner of the gym. *(Fig. 10)* Doug and his wife enjoyed a reunion with Eleanor Curran, the wife of the former bombardier on the *Purple Shaft*. *(Fig. 11)* It was quite an event!

FIRST YEAR OF THE PROJECT:
School Year 1991-1992, Second Semester

January – March, 1992

When school resumed after the holidays, the fifth graders were still talking about the World War II Night. They wondered what to do next. Several asked, "Do you suppose we could find Wanda?" The last letter in the Black Suitcase was dated January 29, 1946 and the fifth graders were now in January 1992. This was still several years before Mark Twain School would have Internet access, so locating Wanda would need to be done the "old fashioned way" with lots of letter writing. Wanda's 1946 letter had a return address of Huntington, West Virginia. Other return addresses indicated Parkersburg, West Virginia. Would it be possible to locate Wanda after so many years? *(Fig. 12)*

The class brainstormed ideas of places to contact that might have information about Wanda. Thoughts included historical

Figure 10: "Donut Dollies" Barbara Gill and Regina Gahr ready to serve refreshments at Mark Twain Elementary School's "World War II Night" December 6, 1991

Figure 11: "World War II Night" participants Eleanor Curran, Doug Richards, Gail Elliott Thomas and Mina Richards

Figure 12: World War II bride Wanda Bee Rich and some of the letters she wrote to her mother-in-law she had yet to meet, Hazel Elliott Rich

and genealogical societies, libraries and local newspapers in both West Virginia towns. The students were divided into teams and each group composed and wrote their letters, then waited to hear results from their inquiries.

One team thought to write to "Unsolved Mysteries" which was a popular television program at the time. A few weeks later, the following form letter was received:

Dear Viewer,

I am replying to your request that "UNSOLVED MYSTERIES" investigate your story.

As you know, each edition of "UNSOLVED MYSTERIES" is limited to only a few stories. Each week's cases must be selected from among the hundreds of worthy stories that come to our attention.

Unfortunately, we will not be able to act on your story at this time. However, please know that our hopes and thoughts are with you.

Thank you for sharing your story with us.
UNSOLVED MYSTERIES
Viewer Mail Dept

During this same time period, the St. Louis newspaper carried an appeal from columnist Ann Landers requesting Valentines for Vets. Leslie, the fifth-grade teacher, immediately gathered supplies so the students could be involved in this worthwhile project. The article gave directions to send the Valentines to the Hines VA Hospital in Hines, Illinois. This gave the students another idea: perhaps Ann Landers could help them find Wanda since her column was carried in national newspapers. A letter was composed, addressed to Ann and included in the box of Valentines mailed to the VA Hospital.

Once again, a letter of regret was received. However, this one was personally signed by Ann Landers! She wrote the following on March 3, 1992:

Dear Mrs. Thomas:

Thank you for your letter of January 30, which the Hines VA Hospital forwarded to my office.

Your class project sounds fascinating and I'm sure your students are enjoying it. What an unusual idea for teaching history and making it come alive for these children.

I wish I could help you find Wanda Bee, but unfortunately, my editors will not allow me to use my column for this purpose. You do, however, have quite a bit of information on this woman including where she lived along with the fact that her parents were well-known citizens of Parkersburg, West Virginia. You might be able to find other relatives who can direct you to the proper place.

Good luck to you. I send my best wishes.

Sincerely,
Ann Landers

The students were impressed that Ann Landers had taken the time to send a personal response, even though she had sent regrets. However, their efforts had already been rewarded!

In the summer of 1943, Wanda's mother had mailed Hazel a copy of the Society page from the *Parkersburg W. VA News*. The Sunday issue for June 13, 1943 told of the recent marriage between Wanda Bee and George Elliott Rich. That clipping, stored for so many years in the Black Suitcase, proved to be the clue to answering, "Where's Wanda?" The clipping stated that Wanda had graduated from Belpre High School in Belpre, Ohio. Based on the information from that wedding announcement in the Parkersburg newspaper, one group of students wrote to Belpre High School. *(Fig. 13)*

Within three weeks, the students in Research Group # 4 received a very welcomed letter which had been written on February 20, 1992.

Dear Class:

Your letter addressed to Belpre High School, Belpre, Ohio, concerning family research on Wanda Bee has been referred to me. I am a retired secretary from Belpre High School, and I am also an alumni from the school.

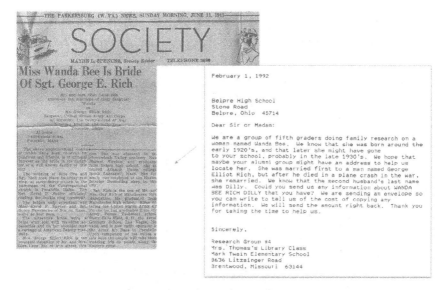

Figure 13: Wedding notice published in Wanda's hometown newspaper 1943 and the 1992 letter fifth graders wrote to her high school hoping for the answer to "Where's Wanda?"

Wanda Bee graduated from Belpre High School in 1940. She was a member of my husband's graduating class. The Class of 1940 had its 50th Year Class Reunion in August 1990. Wanda lives in Huntington, West Virginia, and did return for their class reunion.

Wanda's address is: Wanda Bee Dilley [*address withheld*], Huntington, WV 25702

Good luck to you on your family research project!

Sincerely,
Mildred Chambers

When Gail first saw the newspaper clipping, she had difficulty recognizing the person identified as Wanda. Gail knew she had to prepare the fifth graders for Wanda's physical changes, so she led a discussion about what happens to people when they get older. Comments included, "Their hair gets gray or white and some men go bald. Their skin gets wrinkled. They have to wear glasses and some wear hearing aids. Some people get very thin and seem to shrink while others get heavier."

Once the students were prepared to see the physical changes, they were shown the 50th reunion clipping and the letter with Wanda's address. A cheer instantly filled the library! The students were ecstatic and wanted to immediately write Wanda a letter telling about reading her old letters written in the 1940s!

Whoa…another discussion was needed about what Wanda might have done in the past 50 years. It was known that she had remarried. Did she want to be reminded of George, or was that time in her life too painful to be remembered? How could the students contact her without shocking her too much? It was decided that Gail would write Wanda a letter explaining the contents of the Black Suitcase and invite her to get back in touch if she wanted further contact.

Gail started her letter to Wanda by saying, "You've had no way of knowing, but you've been in the hearts and minds of many people for the past six months." Gail then explained about the remarkable quest the group of fifth graders had begun the previous September. Gail asked Wanda if she would be willing to share more details of George's life with the students.

Wanda called Gail the evening she received the letter and they talked for more than an hour. Wanda was delighted to learn of the World War II project and said she would make copies of all the government correspondence she had saved. On March 14, 1992 she wrote:

Dear Gail,

It was so wonderful to talk with you Tuesday evening. I am sending you the copies of all government mail that I saved. You will notice that I tried to get more information in 1991. The letters George wrote to my mother are still in the package tied with blue ribbon as I found them. Several poems are also included as all were in the package. Share them with your students if suitable, (but I do not want them back).

Also, I discovered some snap shots of my visit to Hazel and Willard. One of your parents with an infant dated 1946, could that be you?

George was born Sept 12, 1921 in Hamilton, Ontario, Canada — Guy and a partner were in the music business! When I bring George's album you'll see his grandparents, friends, costumed memories of the operettas — (he sang bass). Also his 2 cars and many buddies in service.

George was a very happy person and made friends easily. I never saw him angry or upset. We were truly in love with each other and I must tell you I have never replaced that sentimental feeling — of violin music, birds singing and bright blue sunny skies — all because I felt George's love for me. During the war years we never took anything for granted. I wrote to George every day when he went overseas. The quality of our lives together was much greater than the amount of time we had to be together.

Please keep me up to date on your plans for May — and if you have any questions, just ask! I have gathered all my little collection into one box to bring with me. I phoned George's cousin, Ronald G. Snider, who is also my cousin on my mother's side.

He hopes to plan a trip too. My very best wishes to you and the 5th grade students.

Wanda

The students were thrilled when they learned that Wanda had made contact with Gail! Each one wrote a personal letter inviting her to visit in May. Wanda wrote the following on March 17, 1992:

Dear 5th graders:

Your most kind invitations were received yesterday. I am so thrilled and honored to accept your generous offer to meet with all of you in May.

Your interest and research into the life of my husband, George E. Rich has been awesome! A special thanks to Mrs. Thomas for saving that "Black Suitcase" of her aunt, Hazel Rich.

We have so much to talk about and I want to personally thank each of you for your hard work and interest in the events of World War II and discovering facts about George and me.

It is with great pleasure that I accept your warm invitations to meet all of you and Mrs. Thomas in May. I am enclosing a snap shot so you will see how I now look after all these years!

Thank you for your snap shots — you look so friendly in the school room!

Sincere good wishes to all of you,

Your "lost" friend
Wanda

After receiving her acceptance letter, the students began another round of research projects, this time focusing on Wanda's life from the letters she had written in the 1940s and what they knew of George's youth in New Hampshire.

February - April, 1992

While the students were involved with finding Wanda, making Valentines for Vets and later, researching to prepare for Wanda's visit, Gail began a correspondence with another member of the 456th Bomb Group. Fred Riley, a resident of Wisconsin, served as the 456th Bomb Group Historian and the editor of the *456th BG Newsletter*. Pilot Doug Richards had contacted him after his December visit to Mark Twain School and explained the fifth graders' desire for details regarding George Elliott Rich. Fred Riley wrote:

Dear Gail,

Doug has sent me copies of the correspondence and activities in which you are having your class participate. I find it all very interesting and have been able to extract some useful information from Doug's writings.

While reviewing microfilm I ran across several items I wanted you to have. One had to do with the crew of the *Purple Shaft* and pointed out that collectively they were the most decorated crew. [*Editor's note:* The microfilm states, "The crew collectively holds three Silver Stars, three Distinguished Flying Crosses and four Purple Hearts." George Elliott Rich received two of those Purple Hearts. The first was awarded for injuries received when the *Purple Shaft* sustained the gaping four foot hole near the belly of the plane. His second Purple Heart and Silver Star were awarded posthumously.]

The microfilmed item that held the most information was the "War Diary" which dealt with the June 13, 1944 mission to Munich. That document which was stamped "SECRET" totally fascinated the students! The "war diary" gave numerous details about the mission that disabled the *Purple Shaft* and gave official acknowledgment of George Elliott Rich's act of heroism:

Organization: 746th Bombardment Squadron (H); Station: Stornara; Location: Stornara, Italy; Month: June; Day: Thirteenth; "The *Purple Shaft*" seems to have been ill fated from its beginning. Again, as on the 23rd of May, it received a direct hit in the waist. Also, as before, S. Sgt Jerry Krenek was injured. Injured with him this time was T Sgt George E. Rich, Radio Operator.

Over the target, Munich, S Sgt Brown from his position, ball turret, (A/C 489) could see flak bursting excitedly ahead. "Flak-wise" from many similar missions he soon realized that their ship was being tracked. Directly, forward, a burst, and then again. Realizing that a third burst would be near his position in the ball, he unlatched and threw open the hatch door. Wham! The flak hit. The force of the blast exploding just forward of his position, threw him out of his turret and up through the open hatch. A bump on the head and a couple of pieces of flak are his only mementos of this "near-miss."

The boys in the waist did not escape as easily. The flak when it burst, tore away the flooring in the waist. The ship rocking from the blast and feeling the floor give way beneath him, Krenek, (LWG) clutched his safety strap and gun. Rich from the opposite waist position, saw Krenek slipping through the wrent flooring. He threw off his oxygen mask and grabbed for him. Seizing him by his parachute harness, he pulled him to safety. It was then he noticed that Krenek was seriously wounded. Flak fragments had torn into his feet and legs. Rich immediately began first aid. Breathing with difficulty, he attempted to put his oxygen mask back on. There was no oxygen. The system had been smashed by the same blast that had torn a hole through the ship and had wounded Krenek. There was a portable oxygen bottle intact. This, he gave to Krenek, sacrificing his comfort to the greater needs of the wounded man.

Litcher, from his place in the tail, started forward to see if he could help. Rich motioned him back. As Litcher said later, "I thought as long as Krenek was being taken care of, that I had better get back to those tail guns. We would be "Dead Pigeons" with no waist guns nor ball turret if I were out of the tail." He said later, "When I climbed back into my turret, I had my flak suit off and my chute on. You know, the tail was so wobbly, that every little jolt felt as though the tail was going to crack off the ship."

Off oxygen and at lower altitude, Rich who had been too busy with Krenek to notice, realized that he himself had been wounded. Lt. Curran, bombardier, came back to the waist and administered first aid to Rich.

This was the Shaft's last combat mission. Back at the field, Krenek was rushed to Foggia hospital for emergency treatments and Rich with lesser wounds to Cerignola.

Fred Riley sent another document which gave additional information about George's last mission. The following was printed in the August 1944 "History of the 456th Bombardment Group (H)" and read:

> For the 456th Bomb Squadron the 22nd of August was a very bad day indeed. The target was Blechammer [*sic*] South Synthetic Oil Plant and over the target A/C #256 received direct flak hit in the left wing after the rally from the target and flames streaked back the length of the fuselage. The left wing crumbled and the ship fell off to the left and turned over on its back. From here on the accounts differed. Some say the ship exploded, others say it crashed on the ground; some saw nine chutes open, others didn't see any. Nearly all the men on the ship were on their 50th mission and Captain Frederick Hyde, 746th Operations Officer was also aboard.

"History of the 456th Bombardment Group (H)" for the month of April 1945 related more information about that same mission:

> 456th BG in ITALY—When you list the heroes of the war in Europe, don't leave off the name of 1st Lt. Wilson Goodall, a Liberator bomber pilot who is still reported missing in action.
>
> The story of his heroic action on a bombing mission over Blechammer [*sic*], Germany, last August, came to light the other day during a "hangar session"

between a couple of pilots who flew in other planes on the same mission.

Lt. Goodall was flying his 50th combat mission that day, the mission that would have wound up his tour in the Italian campaign.

"I remember the mission pretty clearly," said one pilot, now an operations officer at this base. [*Editor's note:* This may have been Doug Richards who became the Operations Officer after Capt. Hyde was missing.] "The flak was terrific. Lt. Goodall's plane was catching plenty of hell, too, but he stayed in position in the formation and completed the bombing run with the group.

"A few seconds after bombs away a direct hit struck Lt. Goodall's plane in the wing section between the number one and two engines.

"The entire wing burst into flames, and you could tell by the way the plane was bouncing around that he was fighting desperately to keep the plane under control and on an even keel.

"He was cool though and saved us from a possible collision and confusion by quickly pulling the plane out of formation. Then, we saw one, two, three chutes open.

"Almost immediately, the left wing broke into two pieces and the plane, still burning, plunged toward the earth. We lost it in the smoke and couldn't see if any more chutes opened or not, but when last seen he was still trying to control the plane.

"He was a great pilot," the officer concluded, "but we haven't heard a word of him since."

After Gail read the material that Fred Riley sent, she invited him to share his stories with the fifth graders. He made a visit to St. Louis in April, 1992 and spoke to the Mark Twain students. He told of his experiences as a bombardier with the 456th Bomb Group in Italy. As Fred Riley prepared to leave Mark Twain Elementary School, he expressed his appreciation to the students for their efforts in learning about World War II. He commented that he would include a story about the Black Suitcase Mystery in the next edition of the *456th Bomb Group Newsletter*.

April continued to be a busy month for Gail. The provider of the local cable television network announced that she was to be the recipient of an educator award for outstanding use of cable programming in the classroom. Entries in the national competition were judged on the basis of objectives, design, innovation, unique features, effectiveness and benefits. Judges were experts in the fields of education and television.

Earlier in the school year, the students had watched an episode of *Wings* produced by the Discovery Channel. Gail had written a newspaper inquiry wondering if anyone in the St. Louis area had taped the episode that dealt with B-24 Liberators. She made contact with an Army Air Force veteran who had taped the show and he agreed to be a guest speaker at the school. This gunner's B-24 had crash-landed in Holland and he became a German prisoner of war for 15 months. He attended the school's World War II evening on December 6th and met another B-24 veteran who had also previously spoken to the fifth graders. As they talked, they realized they had belonged to the same squadron in England and had flown five of the same missions. They had a mini-reunion in the Mark Twain School gym! [*Editor's note:* This is another coincidence in the Black Suitcase Mystery.]

As part of her educator award, Gail had an all-expense paid trip to Washington, DC and met with the Missouri Senators and Congressmen. Senator "Kit" Bond was so intrigued with the World War II project and its educational applications, he had it entered into the *Congressional Record* on Tuesday, May 19, 1992.

In Volume 138, Number 70, under the heading "Senate" is the title "The Black Suitcase Mystery":

> Mr. BOND. Mr. President, today I would like to recognize a group of outstanding fifth-grade students and their school librarian, Mrs. Gail Elliott Thomas, at the Mark Twain Elementary School in Brentwood, MO. Mrs. Thomas began a project to teach students about the events during World War II. Utilizing a program from the Discovery Channel, students were able to learn about B-24 Liberator bombers. Students studied magazines, military books, pamphlets, military paraphernalia and music — all from the 1940's. In addition, she gave students a chance to have hands-on experience with a black suitcase, which was the inspiration to the project.
>
> The items in the suitcase were memories from the past, and Thomas and the fifth graders at Mark Twain Elementary were able to go back in time. They learned not only about the war, but the experiences of what many families went through of loved ones going to fight for the freedom of their country. All of these experiences and emotions, half a century old, were preserved in this special time capsule. Through the exploration of the contents in the suitcase and their research with books, magazines and veterans of World War II, the fifth graders were able to relive the forties and bring a lot of memories back to life.

Mrs. Thomas and the fifth-grade students at Mark Twain Elementary serve as models for others to follow in developing and encouraging innovative projects for our children's education. The story of the "Black Suitcase Mystery" certainly was of personal significance, affecting the lives of not only the students but also the community of Brentwood. This project has helped to keep the memories alive of our Nation's history and more importantly, has encouraged more student involvement in exciting educational lessons such as Thomas'.

Mr. President, I ask my colleagues of the U.S. Senate to join me in congratulating Mrs. Gail Elliott Thomas and the fifth-grade students at Mark Twain Elementary School for their hard work, enthusiasm and dedication to education. I extend my best wishes to Mark Twain Elementary School for success in all their future endeavors. *(Fig. 14)*

May - June 1992

The day of Wanda's visit, May 22, 1992, finally arrived. It was the 49th anniversary of her marriage to George. The students presented Wanda with a red rose corsage and she showed them the red rose corsage, wrapped in tissue paper, from her wedding day, May 22, 1943! Wanda acknowledged her physical changes by saying "I am whiter, wider and wiser than I was 50 years ago!" and then told about her life with George. She mentioned she was a student at Belpre High School for just her senior year, 1940. The 50th Class Reunion was the only one she ever attended. If she had not gone to that in 1990, it is unlikely the students would have been able to locate her.

Wanda totally surprised Gail by making a gift of all George's medals and citations, the 48-star flag she received in his honor,

Figure 14: Missouri Senator "Kit" Bond and Gail in his Capitol Hill office April 1992

his photograph album and a wooden souvenir box George had purchased for her while on R&R [Rest and Relaxation] on the Isle of Capri, Italy. *(Fig. 15 – 17)* George had intended to bring it home to her after his combat tour was completed. Howard Shields, one of George's closest buddies, knew of his plans so had sent the box to Wanda after George was declared Missing in Action on August 22, 1944. Wanda wanted George's precious things to stay with the Black Suitcase and knew Gail would treasure them and be able to share them with future fifth-grade classes.

Wanda's visit on her 49th wedding anniversary was an emotional day in the Mark Twain School Library. What an unbelievable finale to the fifth graders' year-long study of the Black Suitcase Mystery and World War II. The basic "Mystery" in the Black Suitcase had been solved. The students knew the authors of the letters and why they abruptly ended.

Figure 15: Decorations, medals, patches, and 48-star flag awarded to George Elliott Rich

Figure 16: George Elliott Rich's photo album, Bible, and some of the "sweetheart" jewelry he gave to Wanda 1942

Figure 17: Wooden souvenir box that George purchased for Wanda when visiting the Isle of Capri, Italy on "R&R" April 1944

They had had the fantastic experience of meeting the pilot of the *Purple Shaft*, a man who personally knew George. They had wondered, "Where's Wanda?" and they had found her! *(Fig. 18 – 19)*

Gail and lead teacher Leslie Brann knew they had involved the students in authentic World War II research and, judging from the responses of the fifth graders, it was evident that they were enthused about studying this time period in America's history. Gail and Leslie once again consulted with Mark Twain principal, Jackie Whitworth, and agreed to continue the project into the next school year. More World War II 50th Anniversary events would occur in the upcoming months and could be the basis of more research projects.

As promised, Fred Riley featured the "Black Suitcase Mystery" when he published the May 1992 issue of the *456th Bomb Group Newsletter*. In his introduction, he wrote:

Figure 18: Wanda, age 18, wearing "sweetheart" locket sent by George while stationed in Sioux Falls, South Dakota October 1942

Figure 19: Wanda, age 68, visiting Mark Twain Elementary School on her 49th wedding anniversary May 22, 1992

A most unusual story has come to my attention concerning a number of our 456th people past and present.

In fact it is so interesting and ongoing that I intend to present it in several newsletters. Some of the principles [*sic*] may be at the forthcoming reunion.

It all began on 22 August 1944, over Blechammer [*sic*], Germany (now Ujazd, Poland), a mission of the crew of the *Purple Shaft* flying deputy lead in A/C believed to be 42-78256 named "You Never Had It Better" [Editor: How ironic!] (the crew were not on the *Purple Shaft* that day.) When they were hit by flak and the A/C exploded. [*sic*]

The pilot that day was Lt. Wilson "Goody" Goodall. Captain Frederick W. Hyde, 746th Squadron operations officer was flying as co-pilot and deputy command pilot. Doug Richards the pilot and commander of the crew of the *Purple Shaft* was flying as command pilot in another plane just to the left of "Goody" and his crew.

The story is the result of the death of the radio operator killed in action over Blechammer, Germany that day in 1944, T/Sgt George Elliott Rich.

Let me set the stage with a story that appeared in the *St. Louis Post Dispatch*, 6 December 1991.

MEMENTOS OFFER CLASS A GLIMPSE OF WWII

Brentwood Youths Learn Stories of War: by Margaret Gillerman of the St. Louis Post-Dispatch Staff

The fifth graders at Mark Twain School in Brentwood know that war is more than what's in a textbook. They are finding evidence in mementos from a small battered black trunk that belonged to the great-aunt of school librarian Gail Elliott Thomas.

Among the items in the trunk and other memorabilia brought to the school were homemade Valentines, a tattered Army nurses uniform, a poster of a B-24 Liberator and a wedding photo — all from World War II.

They tell the story of the lives of the Rich family and the nation during times that were terrible but pulled the nation together.

Stories shared by World War II veterans, members of the Brentwood Historical Society and others have also helped the pupils to understand the war.

Tonight, the efforts of the staff and fifth-grade students of Mark Twain Elementary, as well as Brentwood residents will culminate in a "World War II" evening.

In the spirit of the times, guests will eat "World War II" cake, Spam and crackers and drink Ovaltine.

The project has evolved into a history lesson for the entire Brentwood community and others.

The letters and mementos in the trunk belonged to Thomas's great-aunt, Hazel Rich, who saved everything she had received from her son George Elliott Rich. He was a World War II hero who died at the age of 23, (a member of the crew of the *Purple Shaft*) in a crash of another B-24 Liberator in a bombing mission over Germany.

Some of the letters were from George Rich's bride, Wanda Bee. The students saw their wedding picture taken in 1942. [*sic* 1943]

The guest of honor at tonight's dinner will be Douglas Richards, the pilot of the *Purple Shaft*. Richards has also shared his story with the children.

Since the opening of the trunk, the youngsters have sung the songs of war — "Mairzy Doats" and "Boogie Woogie Bugle Boy of Company B" — in the music class. They have learned to knit. They have danced the jitterbug in gym class and designed their own ship's insignias in art class.

When Gail Thomas first opened the suitcase, she was overwhelmed with emotion. She said the last bundle of letters were those marked "Returned, Missing in Action" in 1944. By 1945 there are sympathy cards and finally, a last letter describing the German cemetery where George was buried.

The letters chronicle the times: gas and food rationing, women working in defense plants, censored mail, wounded soldiers, "victory" bonds, and the hopes and fears of family members back home.

The students in-class learning has been supplemented by a Wednesday World War II club and they have learned about service stars and about growing up in the 1940's. "It's amazing how many people have World War II stories to tell and share" Thomas said.

Thomas also learned from a news clipping that the bombardier of the *Purple Shaft*, Dan Curran, was a St. Louis resident. His widow Eleanor also helped with the project. Pleased with the outcome of the project, Thomas says, "My little battered black suitcase has become a treasure chest."

Earlier, when Fred Riley visited the fifth graders in April, he mentioned that the 456th Bomb Group had scheduled a reunion in Milwaukee the first weekend in June. When Gail realized the reunion date was close to the time of Wanda's visit to St. Louis, she and Wanda made plans to attend. Gail, Wanda and Eleanor Curran, widow of the *Purple Shaft*'s bombardier, drove to Milwaukee and had a tremendously emotional weekend talking to men who knew and served with George Elliott Rich and Dan Curran during World War II.

Before discussing the events that occurred during the 456th Bomb Group reunion, it is fitting to share a few comments and a letter that resulted from Fred Riley's article about the "Black Suitcase Mystery." After dinner on the opening night of the reunion, Gail was invited to speak to the membership and share the fifth graders' project. The assembly was impressed and Gail received the following comments in notes written after the event.

From Fred Riley, dated June 15, 1992:

Dear Gail,

Hope you and the other ladies had a pleasant return trip. I wanted to let you know that I have received many comments on your presentation. All were very much impressed and I am sure there was more than a little welling up.

From Walter Jenkins, a World War II pilot who videotaped Gail's presentation at the reunion, a note dated September 8, 1992:

Mrs. Thomas,

I didn't get a copy of our newsletter until I was in Milwaukee so I just glanced at it quickly. The full impact of your story did not touch me until I was there before you — taping you and your story.

Thank you for introducing the 456th to your class of young folks! It seems that with the rapid speed we have been living since WW-2 that many of the things that are done are too soon forgotten. That is now past and we must look forward to tomorrow!

The 456th newsletter story about the "Black Suitcase Mystery" prompted another World War II veteran to write the following letter, dated June 15, 1992, to Doug Richards:

Dear Doug Richards:

I read, with a good deal of emotion, the story in the latest 456 BG newsletter of your participation in the Mark Twain School event.

I have more than a passing interest, as I was the Radio Operator on the plane in which you were flying on the memorable Blechammer [*sic*] mission. I recall vividly the reflection of flames on the wall of my left side waist position, leaning over to see Lt. Goodall's airplane peel away. It was difficult to follow up as we had our own problems resulting in the put down on Vis Island.

The enlisted men on your crew were tented right across a lane from our tent and were the first people that we got to know. They were helpful getting us accustomed to Sqdn affairs. We were not able to get closely acquainted, however, as we only joined the Group in July, 1944.

My mission schedule indicates that we did get a few days stand-down after that mission, but then we were sent right back to Blechammer. Talk about "Hair of the Dog"!

That letter, written by Richard Verdon, had been sent to Doug Richards who forwarded a copy to Gail. When Gail realized that Dick Verdon lived near Kalamazoo, Michigan she began a correspondence with him. Gail had the opportunity to meet Dick during the 1992 holidays because she had family who also lived in Kalamazoo. *(Fig. 20)* [*Editor's note:* This is another coincidence in the Black Suitcase Mystery.] Dick Verdon had the same training and held the same positions on the bombing runs as George Elliott Rich. Dick was another eye witness to the attack that killed George and seven other crew members.

Dick Verdon showed Gail his scrapbook which included a World War II era newspaper clipping that gave more information about the August 22, 1944 Blechhammer mission. Dick had written a note on the scrapbook page which said, "This must have been an Army News release. I don't recall anyone interviewing me."

The article related details about the "put down on Vis Island" that Dick mentioned in his letter to Doug Richards:

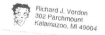

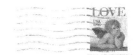

GAIL THOMAS
#7 RITENOUR CT
ST. JOHN MO 63114

Figure 20: Gail and Richard Verdon, WWII radio operator/waist gunner who witnessed the explosion of George's B-24 Liberator over Blechhammer, Germany August 22, 1944

A veteran of 35 missions flown with the 15th air force against enemy targets, T/Sgt. Richard J. Verdon always will remember his first trip to Blechammer [*sic*], Germany, as his "roughest" mission.

"Our plane wasn't touched until we left the target area." According to T/Sgt. Verdon, who is a B-24 Liberator bomber radio-operator gunner. Then the Germans found our positions. The same series of flak bursts stopped our No. 4 engine and sent the plane flying off our wing down in flames. [*Editor's note:* That plane was Lt. Goodall's with George Elliott Rich as radio operator.] The fuel tanks of our No. 2 engine were pierced and gasoline was sprayed over all the plane's fuselage, making it too dangerous to fire our guns even in case of fighter attack. Soon the No. 2 engine was feathering. By this time, the ship had lost both the formation and a good deal of altitude and was flying at 7,000 feet over German fighter fields. Due to the shortage of fuel, the pilot [Doug Richards] brought the plane to an emergency field and just to add the finishing touches a third engine cut out on the landing approach."

Although Dick Verdon did not attend the 456th Bomb Group reunion, Doug Richards and his wife were there. Additionally, someone who knew George Elliott Rich extremely well, Jerry Krenek, and his wife attended. Jerry Krenek, the other waist gunner on the *Purple Shaft* crew, had his life saved by George. As cited earlier, The "Secret" War Diary reported the following details regarding the June 13, 1944 mission to Munich, Germany:

> The flak, when it burst, tore away the flooring in the waist. The ship, rocking from the blast and feeling the floor give way beneath him, Krenek clutched his safety strap and gun. Rich, from the opposite waist position, saw Krenek slipping through the wrent flooring. Rich through [*sic*] off his oxygen mask and grabbed for Krenek, then seized his parachute harness and pulled Krenek to safety.

When the *Purple Shaft* was safely landed, it was discovered that Krenek was seriously injured. Flak fragments had torn into his feet and legs. Krenek's injuries were so severe, he was sent back to the States and spent several years in hospitals and rehab centers recovering from his wounds. *(Fig. 21)* [*Editor's note:* George, for this act of heroism, was posthumously awarded the Silver Star.]

Gail and Wanda joined the *Purple Shaft* table at the reunion and listened to the veterans reminisce about their wartime experiences. Doug explained that the crew of the *Purple Shaft* always flew as a unit until that June 13th flight to Munich when the plane was hit in the belly and barely made it back to the air base. That was the *Purple Shaft's* last flight. After that, each man joined other crews as often as possible in order to come closer to the magic number of "50 missions" and be eligible to return to the States.

Figure 21: George's crewmate Jerry Krenek, flight engineer/waist gunner recovering from injuries after the *Purple Shaft* sustained permanent damages June 13, 1944

One of the saddest notes in the Black Suitcase was tucked inside the sympathy card that Wanda sent to George's mother Hazel on February 16, 1945. In it, Wanda wondered, "Will we ever know what did actually happen?" Wanda had waited from September, 1944, when George was declared Missing in Action until February, 1945 to receive official notice that George was killed on August 22, 1944. That mission was George's 50th and he would have rotated back to the States upon its completion! Accompanying George on that mission were three other members from the Purple Shaft crew: co-pilot Wilson Goodall, Navigator Robert Thompson and Tail Gunner John Litcher.

At the 456th Bomb Group reunion, almost 50 years later, Wanda finally had the opportunity to "...know what did actually happen" on George's 50th mission. Captain Wes Hyde, a West Point graduate and the Operations Officer for George's squadron, was flying as co-pilot on the plane that exploded over Blechhammer, Germany on August 22, 1944. He was at the reunion and spent a morning with Wanda and Gail, plus Doug Richards, sharing his memories. What follows is the transcription of a tape Gail recorded at that time. *(Fig. 22)*

In June or July 1943 we reported to an airfield right outside of Orlando, Florida for special training for Cadre. [Cadre is an outline of people from which you build an organization.] Things were happening so fast all over the Air Corps. They had a hard time finding places for us. We were sent from there to McGloughlin, Nebraska. Then we went to Muroc.

The first crew to report in was Doug Richards'. His crew was #1. We numbered them as they came in. They were all together at Muroc. They had to be in their spaces. They all reported in September. They

Figure 22: WWII B-24 Liberator pilots Doug Richards and Wes Hyde during the 456th Bomb Group Reunion June 1992

had to complete their training, fly their airplane, protect it, defend it, wrap the bombs and all as a crew at Muroc.

We went from there to Hamilton Field, south of San Francisco to pick up our new airplanes. After that, we left for overseas. Each squadron had 17 planes but 21 crews. We put the members of the other 4 crews among the 17 planes as additional passengers.

We got to West Palm Beach, Florida, where we got our orders to go overseas. That was the first time we found out where we were going. We were going to Italy instead of England.

We became part of the 15th Air Force after we got to Italy, Stonara, near Cerignola. We started our runs. We got there in January and the first mission we flew was in early February, as I recall.

I didn't fly with Richard's crew very often, just when it was necessary for the books, for the records, as he was a totally qualified pilot with an outstanding crew. All were well qualified.

I made it clear to my crews that were finishing that I, as their commander, would fly with them on their next mission. So whenever a crew reached 48 or 49 missions, I'd check the airplane myself and I'd go with that crew.

And on those days, I had another reason. Overall, they would be squeamish as they approached their 50th mission. They would be nervous, squeamish. Although they've survived this far, if you looked at it either way, the odds say you're not going to make it through; but then the odds say, if you've made it this far, chances are you're going to complete it.

So I tried to get my missions out of the way. As commander, I was only supposed to fly 1 out of every 4 missions because I was part of staff leadership. So I had flown 4 in a row and had planned to spend the next 5 days in Rome. We had just liberated Rome, and remember, it was a Free City. We never attacked Rome.

So that afternoon, which would be the 21st of August, after the missions were in and we knew what had happened, crews went through interrogation. I had just finished interrogation. Suddenly, Goodall appears in the Operations tent and said, "Captain, the crew has sent me to ask you to take us on our last mission."

I said, "When do you want to go, Goody?"

He said, "Whenever you say, Sir."

I said, "Let's go tomorrow. Let's get it over with." I couldn't go to Rome for 5 days and let them sit on their duffs getting scared and squeamish.

I knew Doug's crew better than any other crew in the squadron because his crew was at Muroc first.

Another point I should have made earlier somewhere, is that early in the combat experience, I think it was Goodall that went to Richards and told Richards he had a premonition that he would not make it. This was early, probably in March, after their first 5 missions. This was before they started receiving those heavy crew losses. They did have more crew decorations than any other crew had. That's just the luck of the draw. They just happened to be in the area of the flak when they went off. Almost all the flak we experienced was barrage fire. Doug told me about Goodall's premonition. Goody and I had not talked about Goody's premonition.

When we were issued our personal equipment, each squadron was issued 4 backpack chutes, as opposed to the chest packs. They were strapped and fitted around your back and shoulders so you could work around the airplane and not be out of your chute. You had the chute with you at all times.

There were only 4 backpacks for the squadron. They were assigned traditionally for the use of the 4 senior flying people: Squadron Commander; Squadron Operations Officer, me; Squadron Bombardier and the Squadron Navigator.

But when we got to combat, we put all the chutes together in one tent. Those backpacks went to whomever, or whichever of the leadership was flying that day. If there was still one, two or three remaining, then the crew who were first in line to get parachutes got the backpacks that were there — out of the four.

The day I flew with them, the 22nd, I took my backpack, the navigator Thompson took another backpack and Litcher, the tail gunner, was in line early enough that he got one and Richards had the fourth one. The rest had chest packs. The chest packs clamp on rings.

As my flying and combat experience grew I began to, of course, think about, "What if..." and "How am I going to get out?" And I had a premonition that I was going to face the exact experience that Goodall had feared...the fire and all. So I sat down and wrote a letter in May or June to my fiancée and told her about the backpack and regardless of what she heard about my being missing in action, should that ever happen, don't give up hope because I probably got out of the airplane safely. She never gave up hope.

So, Goodall came to the tent and I said, "We're going tomorrow." He said, "Fine," and went out and told his crew. Of course, my office had to get to work right away and submit names to fill the holes. I told them who the pilot would be, Goodall. I would sit in the co-pilot seat. Goodall, on his last mission, would be in command. It was his crew. I made that my policy. The crew commander was in charge of his crew, not supervisory personnel along for the ride.

I went up after supper to Group headquarters for an evening briefing at which we were told what bomb loads we would carry, armament, when we would start engines, when we would taxi, when we would take off, the order we would fly in the formation, all that. The following morning, at the briefing for the entire crew, they would tell you about the mission.

The Group navigator and I were standing together and he took me aside and said, "Are you going on a mission tomorrow?" I said, "Yes" and told him why. He said, "Don't go. Don't go." I said, "I've promised the crew we're going tomorrow," which I had, of course. But finally I said, "Tell me where we're going." He said, "No, I can't tell you that." I said, "You can draw a circle on the map showing me the general location." And he did. I said, "I've been up there a number of times, and it was always a milk run."

There was another reason that I set myself up to fly those last missions. I *did* have an inordinate amount of good luck when I flew. We just didn't have accidents. We didn't generally even have flak. They were so far off our altitude that we suffered very little flak damage afterwards.

So I prevailed and we took off. Doug was leading the squadron. He was flying in the right seat and in the left seat was a brand new pilot, a captain who had never seen combat before. So, since he was a captain, I thought I had to check him out as a flight leader. So Doug was showing him how to fly and lead the squadron in the position as the squadron's leader. *(Fig. 23)*

We bombed on the leadership. When the leader's bombs went away, ours went away. When the leader's bombs went away, the lead bombardier was correcting for his course and speed. The bombardiers of the other boxes set the rate so that they would drop their bombs at the same point that the lead bombs went away. The lead bombardier flew the course and we flew formation in that box.

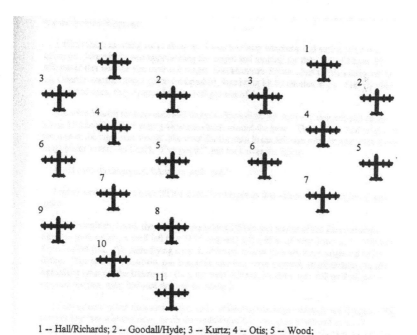

1 -- Hall/Richards; 2 -- Goodall/Hyde; 3 -- Kurtz; 4 -- Otis; 5 -- Wood;
6 -- Shinnors; 7 -- Smith; 8 -- White; 9 -- Dunvannt; 10 -- Maupin; 11 -- Cerretti

Figure 23: Diagram of flight formation utilized on the mission to Blechhammer, Germany August 22, 1944

Doug was leading the high right box and I was on Goodall's crew. We were on the right wing looking right at him [Doug] all the way. As we approached the initial point, which is the point on the map from which you start your bomb run, I reached down for some reason and broke a long standing practice: I put my seat belt on. Normally, we took them off after take-off and never used them again until we got in a traffic pattern. I usually unhooked my seatbelt so I could react quickly and get out. I was being led to do something I didn't plan to do. I began to get serious about this mission about this time. So, as we started the bomb run, I reached down and put my seatbelt on and I knew I was doing something I'd never done before, but I did it anyway. I felt a strange feeling that something else was moving me and making me… really, this is true…and I'm not coloring it either… this is exactly what happened.

I didn't think anything more about it. I was too busy watching and seeing what was going on. Everybody was approaching the target and looking for flak. We did have 8 millimeter flak barrage fire over our target, Blechhammer South. Just to the southwest of us, Odertal, another major place we bombed, was being hit by another wing. Shortly after we dropped ours, they dropped theirs and got out of the way.

We were briefed to drop ours and make an immediate left turn at 5 degrees and fly for about 15 minutes. Then start a slow turn back toward the base. The practice had been that the man in the right seat would take over for the man in the left seat after bombs went away, to give him a rest. So I said, "I've got it," and took over the flying [from Goodall].

I said over the intercom, "Another milk run."

Litcher said, "It's not over till it's over," or words to that affect. Then everything got quiet.

All of a sudden, Ladd, the Group Operations Officer and leader of the Blechhammer mission, took us into a hard left turn, 135 degrees and a dive, all the way to 17,000 feet from 24,500 feet. We were flying a much different course than we were supposed to be flying. That put our squadron, our bombers, our box, over Odertal, an oil refinery, to the immediate west of Blechhammer. Its guns were still hot, its crew was still on their guns because another wing had just finished bombing it.

I didn't know at the time and neither did our intelligence know because we'd already had our briefing that a brand-new, newly-commissioned German gun, a railroad gun, 150 millimeters was at Odertal. It aimed and fired and the first stick of 8 shells came up on my right rear and took off the tip of the right wing. These were gigantic bursts that I'd never seen before; higher than this room is high, much higher than the ceiling. I could hear them explode, they were that loud. What I didn't know was that another stick came up on the left side. The first one of those that exploded near us hit the airplane at the root of the left wing, where the wing goes into the fuselage. It immediately burst into flames.

I was flying the airplane and Goody was resting after the bomb drop. I tightened up on Doug's wing. We were going down. I saw huge shells come up on the left. I turned to look at Doug. Thought I read what Doug was thinking. Goodall and I had not conversed with each other since right after the hit on the tip of the right wing. Then all of a sudden, we got that explosion at the root of the left wing. I said, "One hit the root of the left wing." The left wing started to fold away and I watched it go. I watched Doug's eyes. I knew this was it. I worked the controls a little bit and nothing happened. Goodall left as soon as that shell exploded. The last thing I saw before I tried to stand up and go with him was his parachute, right there under his seat. He never tried to pick up his chute when the plane was hit. He went towards the bomb bay.

Thompson [the Navigator] was standing between the seats at the back, so I could always look over my shoulder where we were. Thompson dived for the bomb bay. He tried to get through the bomb bay. One door had stuck open.

I first tried to get up several times and couldn't and was approaching panic. Then I remembered and undid the seatbelt. By then we were in a tight spin so the centrifugal force threw me up into the canopy [cockpit roof] with my feet towards the back and my head towards the nose.

I saw a great big hole in the windshield. I'd seen a B-17 co-pilot climb out with full gear, leather jacket, pants, the works. I'd actually seen him climb out of that window while the airplane was burning. So I said, "If he could do it, I could do it." I reached for that hole in the windshield and I couldn't move my arms because of the centrifugal force. I looked down and I could see Germany spinning around down there and I stopped and prayed, "Dear God" and the plane exploded.

I felt a big shove. The next thing I was out, hanging in air, with my head to my chest. I've got to get my parachute open. I reached up to my flak helmet and my chin strap almost pulled my head off. I looked down, then looked up and there was the chute. I was blown out of the plane. I saw pieces of airplane fluttering, tumbling.

I looked down and saw one parachute in good shape. I saw another parachute with holes in it way down below.

When I got on the ground, a German national home-guard greeted me and put a rifle on me and said, "Gehen Sie!" [Go!] I got to my feet and folded my parachute. This guy started marching me over to the woods when a noncombatant officer redirected the German. Then the noncombatant was busy and this guy started walking me to the woods again. I knew he was going to shoot me. Again he was stopped and this time he took me to a shack. Thompson and Litcher were in the little shack.

Litcher was badly burned. Holes burned into his chute so he dropped at a much faster rate even though he was small. Thompson was bleeding very rapidly from his right knee. I proceeded to apply pressure and let up. I kept trying to keep the tourniquet on Thompson's leg. Thompson insisted that I loosen the tourniquet and not keep it on so long. I went through the motions to release the tourniquet. I did what I could do.

Litcher and I talked and two hours later in the afternoon while we were waiting to be taken to the hospital, Litcher wanted me to go over and get his ripcord so he could keep it. I said, "Litcher, don't be silly. You know you pulled the ripcord for the chute to open."

Litcher said, "No, I didn't."

I said, "I didn't either." I handed it to him. As far as I know he still has it.

We know that Goodall left without his chute. Litcher or a German guard who spoke some English told me that Goodall's body was found wrapped around the engine. Litcher saw the other men standing still at their assigned locations, unable to move. None of them reached for their chutes. The ball turret gunner was still in the turret. Litcher was extremely unhappy because he had a backpack chute and was able to get out of the plane and the rest couldn't.

While on the ground, Litcher told me, "When you tucked next to Richards's plane you put us in line for the next stick."

We waited for transportation, which by the way, turned out to be a one-horse cart with a guard dog. Along the road somewhere, sirens were heard and an ambulance stopped at the wagon and offered to take me. My back was damaged and I was in pain. But I knew they couldn't do anything about it. That's the last I saw of Litcher and Thompson. Months later, an officer who was with Litcher and Thompson in the hospital saw me and told me that Litcher said,

"If you ever see Hyde, tell him Thompson didn't make it. He lost too much blood." Thompson died that night.

I reached Frankfurt, Germany for interrogation at the Dulag camp. Sagan, Germany was where Stalag III was. The captain of the interrogation became very angry with me because I said I didn't know anything. The interrogator reached down in a file and pulled out a green card. My name and my father's name were on it. The interrogator wanted to make sure each person was a true prisoner of war and not someone dropped behind the lines. The interrogator already knew the names of the crew that had been found.

Years later I asked the Group Leader why he did what he did [changed course] and he said they'd lost an engine. I said, "I've lost engines before and I stayed in formation. You could have stayed in the lead." And I said, "Where was your white handkerchief?" Disabled planes wave a white handkerchief. He didn't answer me.

Gail and Wanda found it very difficult to listen to the details of George's last mission. Having that day described by a survivor of the explosion was very emotional. However, the experience did provide a sense of closure, especially for Wanda. [*Editor's note:* In 2005 Gail obtained information from a Polish researcher connected with the Poland-based Aircraft M.I.A. Project which investigated the crash site of Wilson Goodall's B-24 Liberator. Included was a map of the area and 6 photos, among them the former school where Hyde, Litcher and Thompson were interrogated and the church cemetery where the fallen airmen, including George Elliott Rich were buried.] *(Fig. 24)*

Wanda's opportunity to meet Doug Richards, Jerry Krenek and Wes Hyde, and finally learn what happened on George's last mission ended the quest she had begun a year earlier, in May 1991. [*Editor's note:* This is another coincidence that occurred in the Black Suitcase Mystery. Gail, after storing the suitcase for nine years, shared the letters with her students

Figure 24: German school where prisoners were interrogated and the churchyard where fallen B-24 airmen, including George Elliott Rich, were buried August 24, 1944

and wrote to Doug Richards in May 1991. Unbeknownst to each other, Wanda, Gail and the fifth-grade students were simultaneously seeking information about George Elliott Rich.]

In a letter dated May 20, 1991, the exact same day that the Black Suitcase was introduced to the fifth-grade class, Wanda had written to the American Battle Monuments Commission. She inquired about the exact location of George's grave in Belgium because she wanted to visit the grave site while traveling in Europe. She had to wait until July 11, 1991 to receive a response which said that the Commission's Register of World War II buried on foreign soil did not contain a listing for TSGT George Elliott Rich. Therefore, another agency would be contacted on her behalf.

The second agency maintained the complete Register of World War II Dead and revealed that following the war, by decision of next-of-kin, the remains of TSGT George E. Rich were repatriated to the United States and permanently interred in a private cemetery in the state of New Hampshire. The name of the cemetery where George was interred and the name of the next of kin who made that decision was available, in another agency! A copy of Wanda's letter would be sent to that organization for reply.

Wanda was confused when she received the July 11, 1991 response from the Battle Monuments Commission. She remembered receiving several documents from the Department of the Army, Office of the Quartermaster General after the War ended. The first one, dated 21 September 1948, stated:

Dear Mrs. Rich:

We are desirous that you be furnished information regarding the burial of the remains of your husband, the late Technical Sergeant George E. Rich.

The official report of burial discloses that his remains were originally buried in the Catholic Cemetery at Mechnitz, Poland, but were later disinterred by American Graves Registration Personnel and moved to a more suitable location. I am, therefore, gratified to inform you that the remains of your husband are now resting in Plot EE, Row 2, Grave 40, in the United States Military Cemetery Neuville-en-Condroz, Belgium.

You may be assured that the identification and interment have been accomplished with fitting dignity and solemnity.

The United States Military Cemetery Neuville-en-Condroz is located nine miles southwest of Liege, Belgium, and is under the constant care and supervision of our government and, you may be interested to know, has been designated as a permanent American Military Cemetery, dedicated in grateful remembrance of our World War II Dead.

The Department of the Army has been authorized to comply, at government expense, with the feasible wishes of the next of kin regarding final interment, here or abroad, of the remains of your loved one. Within the near future, our office will provide you with full information and solicit your detailed desires.

May I extend my sincere sympathy in your great loss.

Sincerely yours,
James F. Smith

Major, QMG
Memorial Division

A second letter was written on September 24, 1948 and explained the procedures to follow to determine the final interment of George's remains.

In reply refer to BURIAL OF
T/Sgt George E. Rich
Plot EE, Row 2, Grave 40,
United States Military Cemetery
Neuville-en-Condroz, Belgium

Dear Mrs. Rich:

The people of the United States, through the Congress have authorized the disinterment and final burial of the heroic dead of World War II. The Quartermaster General of the Army has been entrusted with this sacred responsibility to the honored dead. The records of the War Department indicate that you may be the nearest relative of the above-named deceased, who gave his life in the service of his country.

The enclosed pamphlets, "Disposition of World War II Armed Forces Dead" and "American Cemeteries" explain the disposition, options and services made available to you by your Government. *(Fig. 25)* If you are the next of kin according to the line of kinship as set forth in the enclosed pamphlet, you are invited to express your wishes as to the disposition of the remains of the deceased by completing Part I of the enclosed form "Request for Disposition of Remains." Should you desire to relinquish your

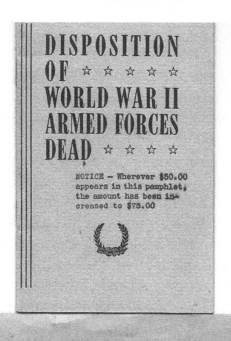

Figure 25: Information sent to Wanda by the United States War Department March 1948

rights to the next in line of kinship, please complete Part II of the enclosed form. If you are not the next of kin, please complete Part III of the enclosed form.

Will you please complete the enclosed form, "Request for Disposition of Remains" and mail in the enclosed self-addressed envelope, which requires no postage, within 30 days after its receipt by you? Its prompt return will avoid unnecessary delays.

After studying the pamphlet, Wanda chose Option I which read: "REMAINS TO BE INTERRED IN A PERMANENT AMERICAN CEMETERY OVERSEAS". She wanted George to remain with his comrades in Europe. George's mother Hazel spent her entire life believing George was buried in Belgium. For 50 years, Wanda also believed that to be true.

Wanda had other government documents that added to the confusion, but also might help explain why George was repatriated to New Hampshire. Soon after enlisting in the Army Air Corps, but before his marriage to Wanda, George took out life insurance. His father, Guy Rich was listed as primary beneficiary and his mother, Hazel Elliott Rich was the secondary beneficiary. George's father was aware that he was named primary beneficiary of the $10,000 life insurance policy.

Wanda knew about the life insurance and in a letter to Hazel, dated March 21, 1945 she explained George's wishes:

> First of all, I want to tell you about George's insurance. His father is to collect it and if anything happens to him it goes to you, because George named you as contingent. This is the way it was made out before we were married and that is how it stands. In my estimation, it throws even a poorer light on Guy's character because now a lot of things take on a new meaning. For instance, when George was reported missing, Guy said he'd never work another day. Guess he knew then what the future held.

Soon after his marriage to Wanda, George completed his will and named Wanda as his beneficiary. It is unknown, but perhaps George changed his life insurance beneficiary when he completed his will. There must have been some legal document executed by George, because Wanda received a letter dated March 21, 1945 stating she was named beneficiary for $10,000 of life insurance. [*Editor's note:* This is another coincidence.

March 21, 1945 was the identical day that Wanda had written to Hazel about Guy getting the life insurance!]

Wanda didn't know the circumstances behind the insurance benefit coming to her, but as a young widow facing an unknown future, she used the money to pay for her college education. She became a home economics teacher, married for a second time in 1947, adopted a son and daughter, earned an advanced degree as a social worker, had a career and retired in 1985.

After being retired for several years, she began her quest to locate George's gravesite in May, 1991. Finally, after waiting almost four months, Wanda received a letter from the Mortuary Affairs and Casualty Support Division, dated September 27, 1991. She then had an understanding of how George came to be buried in New Hampshire and not Belgium as she and Hazel had believed for almost 50 years. She was told that George's deceased personnel file had been located:

> The records state that since you remarried, you lost your right to direct disposition of your former husband's remains. The records also state that in accordance with the order of precedence as established by the Secretary of the Army, the father had precedence over the mother. Since your husband's mother was not awarded custody of her son, his father was the legal next of kin and the person authorized to direct the final disposition of the remains. Mr. Guy A. Rich directed that his son's remains be shipped for burial in the Summer Street Cemetery, Lancaster, New Hampshire. The burial was on or about July 26, 1949.

Imagine Wanda's shock when she got this news. George's father Guy never told the two women who loved George the most that he was buried in New Hampshire. When Guy was granted the power to determine George's final resting place, he did so. Then, perhaps out of spite and resentment over not receiving the life insurance money, he neglected to tell Wanda or Hazel. Hazel died in 1979 believing that her only child was buried in a Belgium cemetery. Both women had been denied the opportunity to visit George's grave.

That September day in 1991, Wanda had no way of knowing that halfway across the country, a group of fifth-grade students were delving into her late husband's World War II experiences. Six months later, when she received and accepted invitations to visit them in person, she was determined to visit George's grave in New Hampshire before meeting the fifth graders.

At long last, in the early spring of 1992, Wanda was able to pay tribute to her beloved George. Wanda and her cousin, Ron Snider, visited Lancaster, New Hampshire and drove to the Summer Street Cemetery. The sexton who helped Wanda find the Rich Family Plot told her that George's grandfather had purchased eight grave sites in the early 1900s and seven were occupied. If she desired, she could have the one remaining site, right next to George! She gratefully accepted the offer. *(Fig. 26)*

Later in May, when Wanda visited the fifth graders, she was able to tell them about her trip to New Hampshire and show them photographs of George's grave. The students asked what her "now husband" of 50 years thought about her being buried next to George. She explained that he had already made his burial arrangements, so she could make her own decisions.

She also shared her upcoming summer plans with the students. She and Gail agreed to meet in New Hampshire and spend two weeks visiting all the places George had known as a child and young man. They would find the houses where he lived in Manchester and Lancaster, visit his schools and spend time in Ogunquit, Maine where he worked during his high school summers. Wanda expressed her sincere appreciation to the students for their year-long efforts in finding her and learning about the people and events in George's life.

July - August 1992

In preparation for their two-week trip to New England, Gail compiled a list of addresses, from George's old letters, and began to make the travel itinerary. Wanda wrote to the historical and genealogical societies in the Lancaster, New Hampshire area and learned that Velma Rich Cummings, one of George's cousins, lived in town. Wanda started a correspondence with

Figure 26: Wanda standing by George's grave in the Summer Street Cemetery, Lancaster, New Hampshire April 1992

Velma and plans were made to visit her in Lancaster later that summer.

In early August, Gail and Wanda met again in Manchester, New Hampshire. Using the return addresses on George's letters to his mother, they located the family residences at 86 Liberty Street and 97 Liberty Street where George spent his high school years. *(Fig. 27 – 28)* Wanda had seen both homes in October, 1943 while on their belated honeymoon, which was George's furlough before being sent overseas. *(Fig. 29)* The drugstore where George worked during high school had changed ownership, but was still a pharmacy. The photography studio where George and Wanda had their wedding portrait taken was still in existence in the same location. George's high school was within walking distance of the main business district and had a memorial plaque honoring graduates who had lost their lives during World War II. George's name was listed among more than 100 other students. *(Fig. 30)*

Figure 27: George's residence at 86 Liberty Street in Manchester, New Hampshire

Figure 28: George's residence at 97 Liberty Street in Manchester, New Hampshire

Figure 29: 97 Liberty Street with photos taken when George and Wanda visited George's father, Guy A. Rich and step-mother Laura October 1943

Figure 30: WWII Wall of Honor at Manchester High School Central in Manchester, New Hampshire August 1992

Figure 31: Wanda visiting her WWII apartment at 747 Pine Street, Manchester, New Hampshire August 1992

During the summer of 1944, Wanda rented a small cottage at 747 Pine Street. *(Fig. 31)* She had moved to Manchester to await George's return and had found work as a clerk in a department store. In a letter to Hazel, a month before George was missing in action, Wanda wrote, "George is very pleased to have a place of our own to come back to."

After exploring Manchester, the next stop was Lancaster where they stayed for almost a week. Gail and Wanda were both eager to visit George's grave at the Summer Street Cemetery. During Wanda's first visit the previous spring, she had obtained the gravesite next to George's and had made arrangements for her own headstone to be installed. In August her headstone was in place with this inscription: SEPARATED BY WAR—REUNITED BY DEATH. *(Fig. 32)* [*Editor's note:* Wanda died November 2, 2010 and is now buried next to George.]

George's cousin Velma proved to be the historian for the Rich family. She had several scrapbooks and photo albums which she shared with Gail and Wanda. Velma was just a few years younger than George and remembered him well. *(Fig. 33)* Most of Velma's neatly trimmed scrapbook newspaper

Figure 32: Wanda viewing her own headstone and George's burial site in the Summer Street Cemetery, Lancaster, New Hampshire August 1992

articles were missing the date of publication, so Wanda and Gail visited the local newspaper office with the hope of finding the archived originals. They were particularly interested in articles pertaining to George's funeral and burial in 1949.

One of the newspaper reporters, Eileen Alexander, became very interested in their quest and the George Elliott Rich connection to Lancaster. She accompanied Wanda and Gail to the cemetery and took photos while interviewing Wanda. Eileen's story was printed in The *Coös County Democrat* on November 11, 1992, Veterans Day. The article entitled "A Tale of Love and War: The Mystery of the Black Suitcase Comes to Lancaster" appeared on the front page of the paper and continued on another page for eight columns. *(Fig. 34)*

Figure 33: George with his cousin Velma Rich taken in Lancaster, New Hampshire sometime during the early 1940s

THE COÖS COUNTY DEMOCRAT

How the week went
Blue smoke means green wood, and there's all too much around.

publishing news & views of L. & other towns of the upper Con

A tale of love and war

The Mystery of the Black Suitcase comes to Lancaster

By Eileen Alexander

LANCASTER—"You don't ever forget your first love," sighed Wanda Bee Rich Dilley, recalling her wartime romance and marriage to World War II airman George Elliott Rich who had been killed in action over Blechammer, Germany in 1944.

Wanda, a retired social worker

now living in Huntington, W. Va., was in Lancaster last summer to peruse old newspaper clippings and memorabilia collected at the Lancaster Historical Society which chronicle the life of George and his family. While in town, she also made photo stops at the Lancaster Elementary School, where George attended for one year when he was

seven or eight years old, and a Evans Market where his grandpa ents lived and he frequently visite while growing up.

On her foray, she was accompa nied by Gail Elliott Thomas, a librar ian at the Mark Twain Elementary School in Brentwood, Mo. Prior to this year, Wanda and Gail had nev er met, but then an amazing coinci dence brought the two women to gether. They have since become fast friends, amateur genealogists and historians in their quest to learn more about the Rich family and the Lancaster area.

The Black Suitcase Mystery

In 1991, Wanda was planning a trip to Europe to visit George's re mains in a World War II cemetery in Brussels, Belgium. She began by contacting the Veterans Adminis tration for information on the exact location of her first husband's grave.

While Wanda was pursuing her plans, Gail began a World War II project with her fifth grade stu dents. The hands-on history pro ject was inspired by a suitcase full of letters and mementos that she had inherited from her aunt, Hazel Rich. The suitcase, which also con tained homemade valentines and a 1942 wedding photograph, chroni cled the life of Gail's second cousin, George Elliott Rich. His mother, Ha zel, had saved everything she had received from her son. Some of the letters were from George's young war bride, Wanda Bee. The last bundle of letters from 1944 was marked "Returned, Missing in Ac tion." These were followed by sym pathy cards and a letter describing the cemetery in Germany where George was buried.

As the students studied George's war-shortened life through the contents of the suit case, one question continued to haunt them. What had happened to Wanda? They even went so far as to contact the television show *Unsolved Mysteries* for assistance in locating her whereabouts.

The puzzle was solved, howev er, when they were able to track her down by contacting her high school, where she had attended her 50th class reunion in 1990. Wan

(Continued on Page 11)

Wanda B. Rich Dilley was in Lancaster recently to place a bou quet of flowers on her first husband's grave. Last year Mrs. Dilley discovered that George Rich, killed in a World War II bombing mis sion, was not buried in Brussels, Belgium as she had believed, but was instead buried in the Rich family plot at the Summer Street Cemetery.

[Staff photo—Alexander]

Figure 34: Article in the *Coös County Democrat*, Lancaster, New Hampshire published on Veterans Day November 11, 1992

In addition to newspaper articles, Cousin Velma had numerous black-and-white photographs of Lancaster that she had taken during her high school years in the 1940s. Seeing them gave Gail an idea which she pursued.

George's elementary school *(Fig. 35)* was still in use and Gail made contact with one of the fifth-grade teachers, Sharon Graham. They discussed the possibility of a pen-pal correspondence between the incoming groups of students at Mark Twain School and Lancaster Elementary School. They made preliminary plans with the idea of involving the students during the second semester of the upcoming school year.

The visit in Lancaster was more than Gail had anticipated. It was wonderful to see the actual places George had written about during his early school days. Before shipping overseas, George helped Wanda get situated near his grandparents in Lancaster. She found work in a string factory and paper mill, but lived in Lancaster just briefly. She had been saving her wages and an opportunity arose to be in California, near George during his last month of stateside training. In November, 1943 Wanda left Lancaster by train and stayed in North Hollywood, with the wife of George's buddy, Howard Shields. The men were granted leave and were able to get into town to see their wives on the weekends. *(Fig. 36)*

Lancaster's Main Street looked very much as Wanda remembered from 1943. They found the building that housed the meat market which George's grandfather owned. In the 1930s George lived with his grandparents in an apartment above the market. Wanda recognized the small downtown diner and the movie theater, which still had its original seats and art deco décor. The week they were in town, the theater featured the World War II era film, *A League of Their Own*. Once again, Gail felt that she was in a time-warp! *(Fig. 37)*

One evening, as they lingered at the diner, Wanda began to reminisce and told about her own childhood and how she

Figure 35: Lancaster Elementary School, Lancaster, New Hampshire August 1992

Figure 36: George and his WWII buddy, Howard Shields, taken in Los Angeles, California 1943

Figure 37: View of Main Street in Lancaster, New Hampshire August 1992

met George. Wanda was born at home on August 31, 1923 in Salem, West Virginia. When she was almost four years old, the family moved to Albuquerque, New Mexico to be near a friend who was being treated for tuberculosis. Wanda's father, Glen Lane Bee, opened the Busy Bee Barber Shop and her mother, Maria Snider Bee, taught grades one through eight in a one-room school house. Wanda went to school with her mother.

Two years later, the family moved to South Lancaster, Massachusetts where a family member owned an apartment house. Wanda was six years old and entered second grade. Her mother enrolled in the Seventh Day Adventist Atlantic Union College and worked in the school library. Wanda's father ran the only barber shop in town. Wanda attended the local schools from second through seventh grade. Her mother became a certified teacher and was assigned to teach English at the college when Wanda began eighth grade. However, the family had to move back to Salem, West Virginia when her grandfather died. Wanda's father took over his dad's barber shop and looked after his widowed mother.

During the next summer, the family moved to Parkersburg, West Virginia because Wanda's mother was hired to teach kindergarten through tenth grade at a Seventh Day Adventist school. She was Wanda's teacher for ninth and tenth grades. Wanda's father opened a barber shop in town.

When Wanda was a junior in high school, she attended the Shenandoah Valley Academy, a private Seventh Day Adventist boarding school in New Market, Virginia. During that year, Wanda's father traded a car for a down payment on a house in Belpre, Ohio which was just across the Ohio River from Parkersburg, West Virginia. Wanda went to Belpre High School for her senior year. She needed just three credits to finish her course requirements, so attended only half-day sessions and graduated with the class of 1940.

Wanda's parents stayed in Belpre until the fall of 1942, then moved back to Parkersburg and rented an apartment. In 1943 they purchased a home at 314 9½ Street in town. Wanda lived with them at this address for most of the time George was overseas.

Wanda first met George during the summer of 1937 when she was thirteen and he was fifteen. Wanda had traveled unaccompanied from South Lancaster, Massachusetts to Akron, Ohio by bus to visit her Uncle Howard Snider and his wife Edna. At that same time, George and his family were visiting his step-mother's sister, Edna Snider and her husband Howard. Wanda and George developed a friendship that summer and corresponded during high school.

In September 1940, seventeen-year-old Wanda began her freshman year at Atlantic Union College in South Lancaster, the same college her mother had attended. She roomed at her former music teacher's home and worked as a "mother's helper" for two children. During school vacations, George's father, Guy would drive to the college and bring Wanda back to Manchester. George and Wanda saw each other four times during that year.

In June of 1941, Wanda went back to Belpre. War loomed ahead and Wanda was not interested in any more college. She wanted a career as an interior decorator and was hired as an apprentice by the Huston Interior Decorating Shop. She acquired upholstering skills and learned how to make curtains, draperies and slipcovers.

A year later, in June of 1942, George met Wanda's parents for the first time, just prior to enlisting in the Army Air Corps. On this same road trip, George had initially driven from New Hampshire to Detroit to see his mother for a week's visit. He and Hazel had not seen each other since 1930. Just before Thanksgiving, 1942, Wanda again traveled unaccompanied by bus to Akron to visit her Uncle Howard and Aunt Edna. A surprise gift was waiting from George: a diamond ring!

By early spring of 1943, George had been promoted to sergeant and had finished most of his military training. He knew he would get extra pay when he gained flight status, so he and Wanda decided to get married. It had been almost a year since they had seen each other and, with the war situation, they didn't know how much time they would have to be to-gether. Their wedding gift from Wanda's parents was a train ticket from Parkersburg, West Virginia to Pocatello, Idaho so Wanda could join George where he was posted. *(Fig. 38)*

During most of the time that George was flying combat missions in Italy, Wanda lived with her parents in Parkersburg. However, in July 1944, she returned to Manchester, New Hampshire and rented a small apartment in anticipation of George's return. Shortly after that, she received the telegram which reported George was Missing in Action and she moved back to Parkersburg to be with her parents. There, she waited for six agonizing months before she received official word that George had indeed been killed.

After the war ended, in September of 1945, Wanda was working as a file clerk in the records room of the Huntington, West Virginia VA Hospital. She realized she had no future there, so enrolled at Marshall College and pursued a Home Economics major because she was still interested in interior

Figure 38: Postcard image of downtown Pocatello, Idaho 1943

decorating. She graduated in January 1949 and began her first job the following September teaching in Barboursville, West Virginia, seven miles out of Huntington. She was responsible for the "school cafeteria" curriculum which taught students how to plan, prepare, cook and serve the noon meals at the school.

While attending Marshall College, Wanda met J. D. Dilley who worked for the American Car Foundry. On June 1, 1947 they were married and later adopted a son and daughter. The foundry transferred the family to various locations in the eastern United States until 1962 when they returned to Huntington, West Virginia. When they were settled again, Wanda began working toward a Master's Degree in Counseling at Marshall College. She was employed as a social worker with the West Virginia Civil Service until she retired in 1985. Five years later, the Belpre High School Class of 1940 held their 50th reunion and Wanda attended. It was that function that enabled the Mark Twain fifth graders to locate Wanda, almost 50 years after her last Black Suitcase letter was written.

Gail was so thankful that she and Wanda were able to stay in George's home town for a week. She had learned so much from Wanda and George's cousin Velma. After they left Lancaster, Gail and Wanda drove to the coast of Maine and stayed in Ogunquit. During high school, George spent his summers there, working at the Chapman House Inn. The inn, known as the Chestnut Tree Inn in 1992, still had the lobby desk that George used when, in 1940, he wrote his mother and said:

> From the letter head, I guess you can see that I'm still at the Chapman House. As I write this letter, I'm sitting at the desk to see that all the guests are OK. *(Fig. 39)*

Seeing the inn and town where George worked was meaningful to Wanda. She could picture him working and having fun with other young people before World War II changed their lives forever.

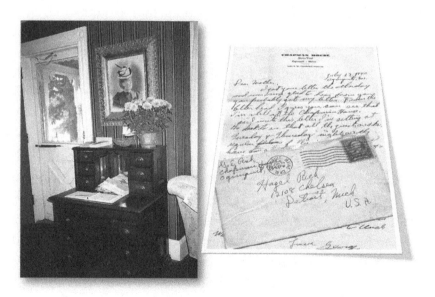

Figure 39: Lobby desk at the Chapman House Inn in Ogunquit, Maine where George worked during his high school summers

When the trip ended, Wanda returned to West Virginia with two weeks' worth of new memories and answers to many questions she had had for 50 years. Gail returned to St. Louis to prepare for a new school year, with plans to include a cross-country connection between the fifth graders at Mark Twain Elementary School in Missouri and Lancaster Elementary School in New Hampshire. She wondered what else might develop from the Black Suitcase study. She had no way of knowing how exciting the upcoming school year would be.

SECOND YEAR OF THE PROJECT:
School Year 1992-1993, First Semester

September 1992

Soon after school started, Gail received information from the United States Department of Defense with information about becoming a World War II Commemorative Community. The brochure stated:

> The 50th Anniversary of World War II Commemorative Community Program is a grass-roots initiative designed to encourage communities, cities, states, federal agencies, military installations and other organizations to thank and honor World War II veterans, their families and those who served on the home front through commemorative events and activities. The commemoration period lasts through Veterans Day, 1995.

Judging from the list of organizations, Gail originally thought a World War II Commenerative Community meant an entire town or city and felt the project would be overwhelming. However, when she learned that schools could also become commemorative communities, plus receive free educational material about World War II, she contacted the Pentagon for more details. She was told that organizations could qualify if they pledged to hold at least three commemorative events or activities annually during the commemorative period.

The Mark Twain fifth graders were already scheduled to be involved in three events a year. Veterans Day would be observed annually by inviting World War II veterans to be guest speakers, Valentines for Vets would be a yearly project, and the culminating activity to each year's World War II and 1940s era research study would be a program held the Thursday evening preceding Memorial Day.

After obtaining the support of additional teachers and staff members, along with community members who had helped the Fifth Graders Focus on the Forties earlier, Gail went forward and applied to have the Mark Twain School become a Commemorative Community. The approval process was estimated to be several months.

November 1992

On Veterans Day, the students had the pleasure of meeting and listening to a local Brentwood resident, Lee Reisenleiter, who had helped the World War II project tremendously the previous year. Mr. Reisenleiter had been a member of the 82nd Airborne Division and had participated in the D-Day Invasion in Normandy, France as well as the Battle of the Bulge. The students knew him well from the neighborhood and developed a new-found respect for him after hearing his World War II experiences. *(Fig. 40)*

A week after Veterans Day, Gail received a boxed package from Lancaster, New Hampshire which contained 25 copies of the *Coös County Democrat* newspaper. The issue had been printed on Wednesday, November 11, 1992 and had a picture of Wanda on the front page with the headline of "A Tale of Love

Figure 40: WWII veteran and Brentwood, Missouri resident, Lee Reisenleiter speaking to Mark Twain Elementary School fifth graders

and War: The Mystery of the Black Suitcase Comes to Lancaster." The caption under Wanda's photograph read:

> Wanda B. Rich Dilley was in Lancaster to place a bouquet of flowers on her first husband's grave. Last year Mrs. Dilley discovered that George Rich, killed in a World War II bombing mission, was not buried in Belgium as she had believed, but was instead buried in the Rich family plot at the Summer Street Cemetery.

The Mark Twain fifth-grade students were very impressed that citizens in New Hampshire were reading about *their* Black Suitcase Mystery! This seemed to be the perfect opportunity to suggest that perhaps they could learn more about Lancaster by becoming pen-pals with the fifth graders who attended George's former elementary school.

The students agreed and worked in teams to write separate sections of a group letter. Once that was completed, they discussed the best wording to include in the finished letter. The following letter to Lancaster Elementary School was mailed in December before the holiday break.

Dear Fifth-Grade Students,

We are writing to you because we would like to know if you want to join us in the "Black Suitcase Mystery." We need to find out some information on George E. Rich's family. We believe his family came from Lancaster. We hope you recognize these pictures taken in Lancaster a long time ago.

If you have time, could you please look at the photographs we have sent you and see if the buildings still exist? The little boy was George Elliott Rich, a relative of our librarian. Is there a river that flows through Lancaster? Maybe you could get information by walking around and taking pictures of the buildings. Also, you could go to the library and gather up other information from other sources. If you can, it would be greatly appreciated.

We have a newspaper from Coös County with an article on George E. Rich. George was married to Wanda and for almost 50 years she thought he was buried in Belgium. George is buried in a graveyard in Lancaster! Do you have any school photos and school records of George E. Rich? If you do, could you send copies of them?

Does this project sound interesting to you? We here at Mark Twain School would like to share some information about the "Black Suitcase" with you! The information we have so far are pictures, newspaper clippings, documents, letters, certificates, medals he got from the Army Air Corps and the flag that was on his casket. We can send some pictures of his things if you would like us to.

Would you like to participate in our "World War II and Focus on the Forties" project? Would you like to exchange pen-pal letters so we can share information about George? Mark Twain has two fifth-grade classes. Mrs. Brann's class has 11 girls and 9 boys. Mrs. Chung's class has 9 girls and 11 boys.

If you want more information, please write back. We'll be more than happy to send you what we know. We hope to hear from you.

Sincerely,
Mark Twain Fifth-Grade Students

On January 12, 1993, the fifth graders at Lancaster Elementary School wrote the following letter.

Dear Fifth-Grade Students,

We received your letter asking us to join you in the "Black Suitcase Mystery." We are very interested in the project and would like to help in any way possible. Mrs. Graham, our social studies teacher, will be assisting us with the project.

The photos that you sent have been identified. All but one of the buildings still exist and we plan to send you information and recent pictures of each.

We are also going to research old newspapers and school yearbooks for additional information about George Elliott Rich's experiences here in Lancaster.

We would be interested in any of the information that you have about George's life and hopefully we will be able to furnish you with some as well. The pen-pals idea sounds great and we look forward to your letters. We have two fifth-grade classes. Mrs. Seppala's class has 13 girls and 10 boys. Mr. Treamer's class has 13 girls and 12 boys.

The "World War II and Focus on the Forties" project is also of interest to us. We have already started interviewing people about this and have become excited about sharing our experiences.

Thank you for this invitation and we accept it with great enthusiasm. We look forward to hearing from you.

Sincerely,
Lancaster Elementary Fifth-Grade Students

SECOND YEAR OF THE PROJECT:
School Year 1992-1993, Second Semester

February - 1993

After the Mark Twain fifth graders received the positive response from the students in Lancaster, they began drafting their pen-pal letters. At the same time, fifth-grade teacher Leslie Brann organized the materials they would need to make

"Valentines for Vets" for the second year. The students' endeavors expanded and they produced a Valentine Video which Leslie described in an article for the February issue of the Brentwood School District's Newsletter.

> "Quiet on the set!" "Cut" "That's a wrap" were only some of the phrases being uttered in the Mark Twain Elementary School's "Studio Five" (otherwise known as the Library) on Friday morning, February 5. The forty-two members of the two fifth-grade classes were combining efforts to film a Valentine video destined for two different audiences, in two different parts of the country.
>
> For the second year in a row, the fifth-grade classes had committed to participation in the annual Valentines for Vets project originated by Ann Landers. The idea continues to seem a natural offshoot to the ongoing "Focus on the Forties/World War II" research project. This year, in addition to the many hand-written messages of appreciation decorated patriotically with red-white-and blue stars and hearts, *(Fig. 41)* the students agreed it would be fun for the recipients of their Valentines to learn of their research projects into the era of World War II, via the video format.
>
> Students next wrote scripts describing the topics they have selected for either individual or team research this year. The scripts were, in turn, turned into cue cards on large poster board, so they could be held just off-camera during filming.
>
> While both Valentines and one copy of the video were sent to a designated Veterans hospital in our

Figure 41: Samples of Valentines for Vets made by fifth graders at Mark Twain Elementary School

area in time for the holiday, still another audience for a second copy of the video was also targeted. The fifth graders are also currently instigating a pen-pal relationship with two classes of fifth graders in the town of Lancaster, New Hampshire. That town has direct ties with the Forties project the students have been researching. It is hoped that seeing the video, and then receiving individual pen-pal letters by each fifth grader will prompt the New Englanders to correspond with these Midwesterners throughout the remainder of the school year.

As Leslie had described, the Mark Twain students' Valentine contributions were sent to a Veterans hospital in time for the holiday. The following letter was written on February 8, 1993 and mailed from the Department of Veterans Affairs Medical Center, Danville, Illinois to the Principal of Mark Twain School.

Dear Principal Whitworth:

On behalf of our hospitalized veterans I wish to thank you and your outstanding students for the "video valentine" sent to our veteran patients.

The video is not only entertaining, it is also informative and brings a personal warmth that touches our patients' lives.

I can see that your students and staff have worked hard and spent many hours producing this tape, and I commend them all on a job well done!

It is obvious that these young people are caring, compassionate and patriotic individuals that now have a better understanding of some of the key ingredients that go into the freedom that all Americans enjoy.

I am forwarding your video tape to our Recreation Therapy department, so that their therapists can show it to select patients for their enjoyment.

Again, students and staff, my sincere thanks for your time, energy and love.

Respectfully yours,
John Howard
Chief, Voluntary Service

Later that same month, one of the fifth graders received the following letter written on February 20, 1993:

Dear Kirsten,

My husband is in the hospital. So I am writing this letter to you, as he cannot write, walk, talk or eat, they have to feed him from a tube through his stomach. Anyway he got your valentine card and he enjoyed it very much. I had to read it to him. He is a veteran from World War II. He has seen lots of things that you or I will probably never see. Anyway, I told him that I would write to you and give you our thanks for sending my husband a valentine card and making him happy for at least one more day.

Sincerely,
Mr. and Mrs. Konazeski

The student wrote back to Mrs. Konazeski and received a second letter written on March 8, 1993.

Dear Kirsten,

First, let me say this, I am so glad that your teachers thought of this project. I hope you learn more about World War II. Second, my husband is a brave and wonderful man. If you'd meet him you would like him.

I am honored that you wanted me to write to you about my husband. Like I said, he is a proud and wonderful man. I hope someday you will grow up to serve our country and someone will want to write about you. But as years go by people forget about men & women who gave so much from themselves to save this great land of ours.

Sincerely,
Mrs. Betty Konazeski

The above correspondence validated to the students and educators that the World War II project was truly touching the lives of others. Later in the school year, Gail received letters from the Lancaster educators describing similar results.

Back in November, when the *Coös County Democrat* published the Veterans Day article about the "Black Suitcase Mystery," the reporter had written:

> While in Lancaster, Gail contacted the fifth-grade teachers at the Lancaster School to see if they were interested in participating in a joint project between the fifth grades in both schools. If the project is put into action it will involve comparing Lancaster then and now, using pictures from old-time Lancaster, researching some of the people in George Rich's family that have been identified by Gail's students; some cemetery and World War II research; correspondence between classes and video tapes.

Sharon Graham, the social studies teacher leading the project in New Hampshire, was contacted by the newspaper for an update on the project. They wondered if the plans discussed the previous summer had materialized. Sharon answered by writing the following letter, which again emphasized the value of the project, not only for the students but the community as well.

> To Whom It May Concern,
>
> I have had the pleasure of sharing a World War II unit with Mrs. Thomas and her fifth-grade students. It has proven to be a unique and exciting project for all involved.

Through Mrs. Thomas' unit, which is based on the contents of her relative's black suitcase, my students have become active participants in uncovering additional information on the life of her relative, George Elliott Rich. Although Mrs. Thomas lives in Missouri, we found that she has a common bond with Lancaster, New Hampshire. My students have found it challenging and rewarding to investigate George Elliott Rich's life and to share that information with Mrs. Thomas and her students at the Mark Twain School. Mr. Rich's grave site was visited by my students and stone rubbings were sent to Mrs. Thomas' students. A video of the present day Lancaster was completed to show the Mark Twain students how George Elliott Rich's community now looks. Old photos, from the black suitcase, were sent to us from Mrs. Thomas' class so we could show the comparison from 1930 to today.

It was also very exciting for the students to discover how relevant World War II was to them. Their investigations found that many of their grandparents, friends, and neighbors had World War II history to tell. This made the history real to them. They became motivated and wanted to share their information with others.

We also participated in the Valentines for Vets program along with the Mark Twain School. Correspondence took place between two veteran hospitals and one veteran nursing home. My students have gained an appreciation for all veterans.

Along the way of gaining this information, friendships have been formed and an exchange of letters, pictures, and videos have taken place between two fifth-grade classes. This has been a wonderful experience.

Sincerely,
Sharon Graham

While the Mark Twain students were making their Valentines for Vets and filming their video for the Lancaster fifth graders, official word was received regarding the application to become a World War II Commemorative Community. On February 15, 1993 Colonel Charles Kramer, Director of Commemorative Communities, Department of the Army wrote the following letter.

Dear Mrs. Thomas

Your committee's application has been received and reviewed, and it is with great pleasure that we notify you that the MARK TWAIN ELEMENTARY SCHOOL has been officially designated as a World War II Commemorative Community.

Your plans for commemorative events are exciting and we look forward to hearing the results of your endeavors throughout the commemorative period.

The official Commemorative Community Certificate of Designation, personally signed by the Secretary of Defense, is enclosed along with the distinctive World War II Commemoration Flag.

We have also provided the Department of Defense 50th Anniversary of World War II Commemoration lapel pin; one for each committee member designated in your application. We hope that you will have a

suitable presentation ceremony and that each individual will wear the pin proudly throughout the
commemorative years.

Again, we are proud to have the MARK TWAIN
ELEMENTARY SCHOOL join us in honoring
those men and women who sacrificed so much for
our country that we might live in peace today.

Very respectfully,
Charles J. Kramer

When the students began to plan a "suitable presentation
ceremony" they wondered what the commemoration committee expected. Gail made a phone call to the committee's
headquarters in the Pentagon and asked if St. Louis had
other organizations with the same designation. The thought
being, those groups might want to participate in the school's
ceremony. While on the phone, she obtained the names of
other committee chairmen in the St. Louis area plus some
thrilling news. She was told that further investigation had
been conducted which revealed that Mark Twain School was
the *first elementary school in the United States* to be designated
a World War II Commemorative Community. That esteemed
status would prove very advantageous in the years ahead.

The Mark Twain fifth graders were well into the second year
of commemorating World War II by this time and had received
a tremendous amount of positive publicity in the community.
However, there were a few critics of the project and one of them
was Gail's own mother! First Lieutenant Emily Dill had served
four years in the United States Army Nurse Corps during
World War II. On a troop ship traveling to Iceland in 1942,
she met First Lieutenant Donald Elliott. They were married
in Tenby, Wales in 1944 and soon after, the newly-promoted
Captain Donald Elliott supported the D-Day Invasion of

northern France. *(Fig. 42)* Emily completed her military tour of duty in Ohio, while Donald found himself in the Battle of the Bulge and did not return to the States until after the German Army capitulated in the spring of 1945. When the war was over, Donald remained in the United States Army and the couple thought about starting a family. They named their first born child, a daughter, Gail Elliott.

Gail's mother, Emily, was extremely proud of her military service and kept asking, "When will the women be included in the Black Suitcase story?" Gail would explain that the project was based on "George's story" and she couldn't contrive a

Figure 42: Portrait of Gail's parents Lt. Emily Dill Elliott and Capt. Donald C. Elliott taken during World War II

connection. Gail knew of her mother's military service and was honored that she had served. However, since World War II was such a huge topic, Gail needed a way to stay focused on topics that were connected to the Black Suitcase story in some way. She told her mother that if an Army Nurse correlation was found to George and the 456th Bomb Group, women would be in the story.

Another critic of the World War II study was a Mark Twain parent whose daughter was a fourth-grade student. That mother wondered why the Tuskegee Airmen were not included in the project. In a letter dated March 6, 1993, she expressed her concerns:

Dear Mrs. Thomas:

In reading the latest *Principal's Newsletter*, I noticed that Mark Twain Elementary School received a Commemorative Community designation from the United States Department of Defense. This is an honor the school should be proud of. Once when I was at the school for an open house I noticed the World War II display you had. I remember when I saw it I wondered why there was no acknowledgement or recognition of the African-American contributions to the war. There are probably a lot of students who could contribute if they were asked.

For example, did you realize that Kareen McNeal's grandfather (my father) was a war hero who received the Distinguished Flying Cross medal? He was one of the Tuskegee Airmen and is featured in a book title Lonely Eagles: The Story of America's Black Air Force in World War II, pictured on the mural at the airport and in the display at the St. Louis

Science Center. During the month of February and March many McDonald's restaurants are using place mats that feature a portion of the mural that happens to have Kareen's grandfather's picture on it. *(Fig. 43)*

Are you aware that the Tuskegee Airmen were the first African-Americans to be allowed to fly for the U.S. Army Air Corps. They were an experimental group that dispelled many of the myths that existed. They were one of the main reasons the military integrated. The Black Repertory Theater is currently performing a play about the Black Eagles and plans are in process for a movie to be made about these men and women and their contributions.

Figure 43: Tuskegee Airmen section of the Black Americans in Flight mural located at Lambert International Airport, St. Louis Missouri

I do not think such an oversight was intentional but it is a significant and damaging oversight none the less. The fact that you did not show any African-Americans suggest that they made no contribution. This is not true. Your display really is not complete unless you have representation of the contributions made by women and African-Americans. I would be willing to provide pictures, a copy of the book or, any assistance you may want. If you ever wanted speakers for a program, there are St. Louis Tuskegee Airmen around who would be available. And, I bet if asked, there are other children who probably have something they could contribute.

I believe all groups have contributions they have made no matter what the subject. You are usually very good at requesting input from the pupil population. If a request was made and I overlooked it I apologize. Whoever missed the communication, let's correct this.

Sincerely,
Kalyn Brantley-McNeel

Gail received Mrs. Brantley-McNeel's letter on March 9, 1993 and wrote this reply:

Dear Mrs. Brantley-McNeel,

I received your letter, dated March 6, this afternoon. I appreciate your interest in Mark Twain's World War II project which we call "Fifth Graders Focus on the Forties." Next year, when Kareen is a fifth grader, I hope she will choose to do a personal research project on her grandfather.

The display you mentioned seeing during Open House contained the items I've collected over the past two years on my own family. When I started the project, which began with a collection of old letters written by my father's cousin, I knew nothing about the Army Air Corps. I couldn't even have identified a B-24 Liberator! Now, I own books, posters, videos and models of that bomber.

I know there have been a few times when I have offended my own mother when I share new B-24 information with her. She has reminded me that both she and my father served in the Army during World War II. I remind her that, just like the war itself, this project is huge.

I spend the first few months of each year teaching the fifth graders how to do primary research. They are taught how to look for clues in documents their families have in their own homes. They then choose a topic of their own interest, including personal family research if they desire. Tomorrow, the fifth-grade students are walking to the Brentwood Public Library to become familiar with that library's references. Students are taught how to find the resources they need for their particular topics. Since I purchase everything for this project with my own personal funds, I continue to focus only on the Fifteenth Air Force and the Home Front, the subjects included in the old letters which began this project.

As my research on the Fifteenth Air Force has developed, I have learned that the Tuskegee Airmen flew Fighter support for the Air Wing in which my relative served. There's only so much I can do during the school year, so I have a trip planned to Alabama next July. I will spend time at the Air Force Research Center in Montgomery, Alabama and also visit Tuskegee.

The fifth-grade teachers and I let the topics evolve naturally. If I have been fortunate to meet someone in the community who can offer us personal insights into the World War II era, the fifth-grade students are the ones who write the letters and invite that person to be a guest speaker.

Next week, in honor of Women's History Month, a member of the Army Nurse Corps will speak to the students. I met this woman last Labor Day when she saw my display at Brentwood's Maddenfest. As a guest speaker she will provide one of the fifth-grade boys with additional information needed for his project because his grandmother was in the Army Nurse Corps. (It has also smoothed things with my mother because I have been asking her about her experiences as an Army nurse).

In preparation for next year's Tuskegee focus, I saved a newspaper clipping with a photograph of three Tuskegee Airmen: Sgt. John E. Ware, Maj. Lewis J. Lynch, and Capt. Christopher Newman. Next autumn, the fifth graders will be tasked with finding the addresses of these men, composing letters explaining our project and inviting them to visit Mark Twain. Hopefully, one or more will be able to speak to the fifth graders.

I will welcome your help in developing this phase of "Fifth Graders Focus on the Forties." As I prepare for the Alabama trip, I would like to know if anything remains of the Tuskegee Airfield. Have any of the veterans you know recently visited the area? Would there be a veteran in the Tuskegee area who might act as a guide to the old air base? Any leads you or your friends might offer will be appreciated.

I hope this letter has helped explain our project in more detail. Each year it continues to grow. Each year it is different, depending on the interests of the students. Next year it will contain information on the Tuskegee Airmen because they are part of the 15th Air Force story and I am the one researching that topic. I will welcome any material you might want to share.

The day of the Mark Twain World War II Commemoration Ceremony arrived on March 11, 1993. A school-wide assembly with all grade levels and community residents in attendance was held with members of the local VFW posting the colors. Active duty military personnel from the Army Aviation and Troop Command and ROTC advisors from Washington University assisted with the impressive program. Mark Twain School received a Certificate of Accomplishment and a Commemoration Banner which flew over the school's playground until 1995. The students made an exhibit and shared it with the large audience who attended the ceremony. The display highlighted the Black Suitcase, some of its memorabilia and the growing collection of awards their World War II study had received. *(Fig. 44 – 45)*

April 1993

A month after having the exchange of letters about the Tuskegee Airmen, Gail was able to join the 456th Bomb Group

Figure 44: Mark Twain School celebration acknowledging the designation of being the first elementary school in the United States to be a World War II Commemorative Community March 11, 1993

Figure 45: Display of awards received and memorabilia from the Black Suitcase March 1993

when they attended their 50th Reunion at the World War II airbase near Foggia, Italy. While roaming the grounds of the old airbase, she overheard several veterans discussing their missions and one said, "We always felt better when the black pilots flew fighter support for us!" Gail asked for details and was told that black fighter squadrons were stationed about 50 miles north of the 456th Bomb Group. This was fascinating information. She had found a direct link between George's bomb group and the Tuskegee Airmen.

When she returned from Italy, Gail started researching the Tuskegee Airmen in earnest. She learned that the 332nd Fighter Group, often referred to as the Fighting Red Tails was based at Ramitelli, Italy and was part of the 15th Army Air Force. The 332nd performed well as bomber escorts, often being requested by bomber pilots because of their insistence on not abandoning the bombers.

Gail found a book in a library's juvenile section that contained the same information she had been reading in adult references. The book described the achievements and combat proficiency of the Tuskegee Airmen and would be easily understood by fifth-grade students. All the books discussed an important mission which occurred on June 9, 1944. The 332nd Fighter Group flew its first bomber escort mission over Germany. They escorted B-24 Liberator Bombers on a mission to Munich. During that mission, four Tuskegee Airmen shot down five enemy fighters. These were the first aerial victories of the 332nd Fighter Group.

Gail wondered if the *Purple Shaft* had flown a mission on June 9th and, if so, where? Pilot Doug Richards had given her a copy of his Flight Record and she noted that the *Purple Shaft* had also flown to Munich on June 9th. The 456th Bomb Group had had Fighter support from the Tuskegee Airmen on that historic and crucial mission! [*Editor's note:* This is another coincidence in the Black Suitcase Mystery!] *(Fig. 46 – 47)*

Figure 46: Flight crew of the *Purple Shaft* including George Elliott Rich pictured last on the lower right

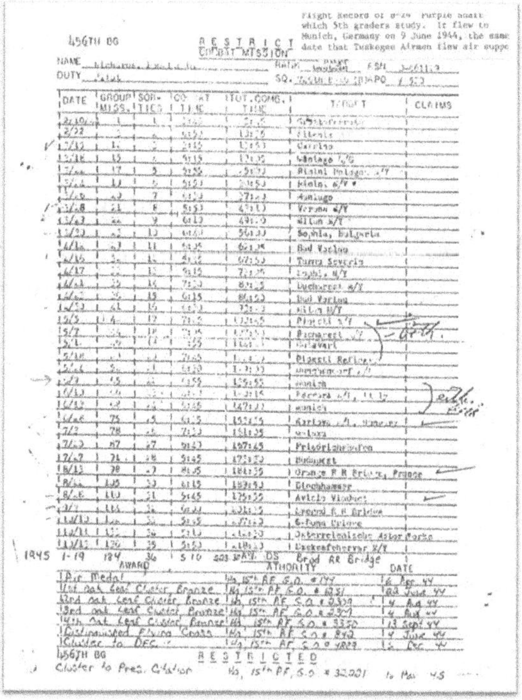

Figure 47: Flight record of the missions flown by Pilot Doug Richards while commanding the *Purple Shaft* B-24 Liberator

May 1993

Another development occurred during the spring of 1993. Earlier in the school year, Gail had the students view an episode from *A&E's Our Century* titled "All the Fine Young Men" which depicted bomber crews flying over Europe during World War II. Gail became the recipient of another educator award for using that documentary film footage provided by cable television networks. The award ceremony and luncheon took place on May 24, 1993 at the National Headquarters of the American Legion in Washington, DC. Gail invited the Director of the World War II Commemoration Committee, Colonel Charles Kramer to be her guest. He attended the event and brought the Committee's Public Affairs and Education Officer, Major Phyllis Phipps-Barnes, who later wrote an article about the Black Suitcase Mystery. The story was included in the summer 1993 edition of the *World War II Dispatch* newsletter *(Fig. 48 – 49)* which was distributed to over 5,000 World War II Commemorative Communities across America. The World War II project that started with a small, battered Black Suitcase filled with old letters was now getting national attention.

July 1993

Gail made her planned trip to Maxwell Air Force Base near Montgomery, Alabama in mid-July and spent a week at the Air Force Historical Research Agency. Her goal was to find and copy the original records of the 456th Bomb Group. She was particularly interested in the June 9, 1944 mission to Munich, Germany which had Fighter support from the Tuskegee Airmen. She wanted to find official documentation which supported the information she had gathered from books about the Tuskegee Airmen. Additionally, she hoped to find records dealing with the August 22, 1944 mission to Blechhammer, Germany which cost George Elliott Rich his life.

The Unit History of the 456th Bombardment Group for the period 1 June to 30 June 1944 reported the following:

World War II **Dispatch**

Vol. II, No. 2   *"A Grateful Nation Remembers"*   Summer 1993

President Clinton honors America's veterans

By SSgt. Teresa K. Jameson
Editor, World War II Dispatch

President Bill Clinton honored America's World War II veterans by signing a proclamation declaring May 31-June 7 as the Week of the National Observance for the Commemoration of the 50th Anniversary of World War II.

"As we observe the 50th anniversary of World War II, our country must remember and honor the millions who defended democracy and defeated aggression," Clinton said.

"The freedoms we enjoy today are results of our victory over aggression, and the efforts the United States makes today to work with all other nations who love and believe in freedom are a testimony to the wisdom of the lessons learned then," he said.

"During this commemoration, Americans of all ages must also remember those who gave their lives and dedicated themselves in other wars so that our nation could remain free and strong; so that the deeds, the commitment, and the

See MEMORIAL DAY, page 15

President Bill Clinton signs a proclamation on the National Observance of the 50th anniversary of World War II during a ceremony at the White House, Memorial Day. (Photo by SSgt. Teresa K. Jameson)

Figure 48: Newsletter distributed to more than five thousand WWII 50th Anniversary Commemorative Communities throughout the United States July 1993

Teacher's efforts earns education grant

By Maj. Phyllis Phipps-Barnes
Deputy Director
Public Affairs and Education

Gail Thomas, librarian of Mark Twain Elementary School in Brentwood, Mo., which is a Commemorative Community School, came up with an award-winning idea. Her fifth grade project, "In Touch With Our Past," earned a National Teachers Grant from Arts and Entertainment cable television network. Her 225 students viewed an A&E program, "Our Century: All the Fine Young Men," to increase their awareness of the magnitude of the U.S. bombing raids over Germany during World War II, the comradery of the bomber crews, and the emotional, as well as physical, demands upon Army Air Force personnel.

Thomas' program had three phases: The Black Suitcase Mystery (20th Century History), A Twig on the Family Tree (Genealogy), and Focus on the Forties (Research Project).

The Black Suitcase Mystery project began with Thomas' father's cousin, George Elliott Rich, who joined the Army Air Corps and wrote many letters to his mother that were kept in a small, black suitcase. Shortly before George left for Italy he married Wanda.

The black suitcase containing letters from George Elliott Rich and a photo of George and Wanda. (Photos by Maj. Phyllis Phipps-Barnes)

Tragically, he was killed on his 50th--and what would have been his last--mission over Germany. The fifth graders read first-hand experiences from the war zone and the home front. Also, members of the Brentwood Historical Society shared their personal stories and experiences with the students.

After studying and learning much about the war, the students wondered what happened to Wanda. They set out to answer the question, "Where's Wanda?" Using genealogical skills during the second phase of study, they tracked her down through her high school. She had attended her 50th reunion. The children wrote to Wanda asking her to contact them if she wanted more details on their project. She did! On what would have been her 49th wedding anniversary, Wanda met with the fifth graders at Mark Twain.

Thomas and Wanda then attended a reunion of George's 456th Bomb Group and learned first hand from fellow crew members the details of George's death and his acts of heroism for which he earned the Silver Star.

The story continued when Thomas and Wanda traveled to George's hometown in New Hampshire and a fifth grade class. Unbeknownst to Wanda who remarried, George's family had moved his body from a cemetery in Belgium to the United States in 1949. As it turns out, the last remaining grave in an eight-site family plot--right next to George--is unoccupied. Now it belongs to Wanda as she plans to be buried next to her first love. Her marker

(From left) Col. Charles Kramer, director, Commemorative Community Programs; Gail Thomas and Seymour H. Lesser, executive vice president and chief financial officer, A&E network, at the A&E awards luncheon in Washington, D.C.

has the inscription: "Separated by War; Reunited by Death."

The fifth graders back in Missouri continued with phase three, "Focus on the Forties," and became involved in semester-long research projects. Military books, magazines and pamphlets of the 40s, uniforms, patches, medals, music, and documentary film footage were used to learn more about the period of the last world war. In April Thomas also attended the 456th Bomb Group's reunion in Italy and in May she was honored along with seven other educators at an A&E awards luncheon in Washington, D.C.

What's next for Gail Thomas? She learned recently that the Tuskegee Airmen, the famous black pilots, flew fighter support for the 456th. She is now planning a trip to Tuskegee, Ala., this summer to do more research on that famous group of aviators and will undoubtably invite some St. Louis members to visit Mark Twain fifth graders next fall.

5

Figure 49: Article about the Black Suitcase Mystery printed in the *World War II Dispatch* newsletter July 1993

MUNICH BAYERISCHE MOTORENWERKE
9 JUNE 1944

Due to weather the secondary target, Munich East M/Y, was bombed by the pathfinder method. 34 aircraft dropped 72.9 tons of 1,000# GP's and 100# incendiaries on M/Y. 20ME-109s were seen but no encounters reported. Flak was intense, accurate and heavy. Results not observed.

The War Diary of the 745th Bombardment Squadron, within the 456th Bomb Group, reported the most details about the June 9, 1944 mission.

Today's target marks the beginning of bigger and better bombing areas to the north, namely: GERMANY, itself. We were briefed on the Bayerische Motorenwerke (aircraft engine factory) at MUNICH, Germany, but due to heavy under cast we dropped in the MUNICH east marshalling yard, instead. Each aircraft carried 6 x 1000# G.P. bombs. The results of the bombing were visually limited, due to cloudiness. However, it is reported that bombs fell in the built-up areas southeast of the marshalling yard, as well as northeast of the target—where hits were made on the important rail line running to Ismaning. The flak was intense, accurate and heavy—as was expected. It was multi-colored, with black, red and white bursts. The enemy fighters which chose to come up and meet our P-47 escort were in the minority—only about thirty-five. The mission was completed successfully, with all aircraft returning home by 1300 hours; no casualties. The much dreaded German homeland fortifications were not too bad after all. No milk run, however! A well-deserved two credit mission.

The *History of the 746 Bombardment Squadron* reported the following:

> MISSIONS: During the month of June 150 sorties and 16 missions were flown. Enumerated in chrono-logical order with appropriate comments as to target, nature of operation, and the result of the mission, they are:
>
> 9 June. Target—Munich, Germany. Flak was intense, accurate, and heavy. There were no enemy aircraft encountered. Results were satisfactory.

The War Diary of the 747th Bombardment Squadron recorded:

> 9 June 1944 The target for today was the MUNICH Bayerische Motorworks in Munich, Germany. Nine (9) aircraft of this squadron participated in today's mission. The bomb load was forty (40) 100 lb. incendiaries per aircraft. Many of the crews reported fires in the target area but due to a cloud cover over the target, accurate observations could not be made. Over the target area, the flak was intense, accurate and heavy. Several enemy fighters were seen along the route and over the target area but none were encountered.

Once Gail had the official reports from George's 456th Bomb Group and knew they participated in the June 9th mission to Munich, she researched the Tuskegee Airmen. Within the "Narrative Mission Reports" of the 332nd Fighter Group,

Gail found the following for June 9, 1944 which pertained to Mission Number 3 of the 301st and 302nd Fighter Squadrons. The formation leader for the 301st Squadron was Colonel Benjamin O. Davis Jr.

> Mission and Target: To provide penetration escort for the 5th, 57th, 304th, 49th, 55th Bomber Wings to the Munich Area.
>
> AIRCRAFT AND CHRONOLOGY: 39 P-47's took-off from Ramitelli A/D at 0700 hours. 4 RETURNED EARLY. Escort and 2 reached R/V point with Bombers, went as far as Trieste and got sorties at 0830: 35 penetrated to Dolsach at 0925 hours. 34 down at base 1240 hours. 1 missing.
>
> ROUTE: Base to line R/V with bombers to Dolsach and return to base.
>
> RENDEZVOUS, FORMATION, AND ASSAULT: R/V as briefed met bomber formations as 22,000 feet at 0830. Bombers were on time-bomber formation was reported as good with the exception of 4 stragglers. Fighter formation was spread out to cover the large bomber formations.
>
> FORMATION LEADERS AND FLIGHT LEADERS: 301st Fighter: Col Davis, Lt Cisco, Lt Faulkner and Lt Covan. 302nd Fighter: Lt Jackson, Lt Bussey, Lt Pruitt and Lt McGee.
>
> RENDEZVOUS was at 20,000 feet. It is believed that it would have been better at 25,000 feet because it would have allowed more freedom of action for the fighters in moving from one formation to the other.

Thus it would have enabled the fighter to afford better protection to the bombers. It was also noted that although the bomber formation was good, there were too many to be covered by two fighter squadrons.

From the declassified June 1944 "War Diary" of the 301st Fighter Squadron, 332nd Fighter Group this information was obtained:

> 9 June, 1944: The Squadron's third operational mission in P-47's was very eventful. Enemy planes were met for the first time. LT. Funderburg received credit for two enemy planes shot down. The first victories for our squadron.

From the declassified "Historical Records" of the 302nd Fighter Squadron, also within the 332nd Fighter Group:

> The missions of greatest importance were the penetration escort to the Munich area on June 9 and the strafing mission in Northern Italy on June 25. In each instance, the maximum effort was given and the targets were of utmost importance in our efforts to halt the supply line of the enemy. The penetration escort was the initial encounter with the enemy of our squadron since the introduction of the P-47 type of aircraft. Our pilots destroyed three (3) of the enemy aircraft encountered without loss to any of our personnel.

The 302nd Squadron's "War Diary" gave more information: The ninth of June proved to be a historic day in the records of the squadron. On an escort mission enemy A/C were encountered for the first time and the pilots met their first test in a meritorious manner. Three enemy A/C were shot down. The victorious pilots were 1ˢᵗ LT. Melvin T. Jackson, 1ˢᵗ LT. Wendell O. Pruitt, and a victory was shared jointly by LT's Green and Bussey. The sqdn. suffered no losses.

Gail was pleased with her success at finding documentation which supported the speculation that the Tuskegee Airmen and the *Purple Shaft* were together on the June 9, 1944 mission to Munich, Germany. She looked forward to a meaningful observance of Veterans Day and hoped it would include a St. Louis veteran who had flown with the Tuskegee Airmen.

THIRD YEAR OF THE PROJECT:
School Year 1993-1994, First Semester

September 1993

The new school year had barely begun when Gail received the first of two intriguing phone calls. Both calls resulted from interest generated by the article published in the summer issue of the *World War II Dispatch* dealing with the Black Suitcase Mystery. The *Dispatch* was circulated to more than 5,000 World War II Commemorative Community agencies in the country and was seen by a Navy officer in Washington, DC.

United States Navy Commander Eric Berryman called to ask Gail if the fifth graders would want to know the "other side of the story." When Gail asked if he meant the Navy involvement rather than the Army Air Corps, he replied, "No, I was a young child living in Berlin when the American planes repeatedly bombed the city." He thought the students might want to know what his experiences had been during World War II. *(Fig. 50)*

On September 3, 1993, Commander Berryman wrote the following letter:

Dear Mrs. Thomas,

As I explained in our conversation on the telephone, the *Dispatch* article describing your World War II project got my attention, and I was moved to consider sharing another kind of view with your students,

Figure 50: Erik Juergen Karl Dietrich, later known as Eric Berryman, as a young boy dressed in partial uniform of a German Wehrmacht soldier near Berlin, Germany 1943

the view of a small boy on the receiving end of what those Army Air Corps bomber crews were sent to deliver to Germany. In no way is this intended to deflect from the heroism of those airmen, or of the rightness of the cause they so willingly risked their lives for. World War II was unarguably a struggle of light against darkness, good against evil. I celebrate the deeds of your late cousin and those of his compatriots who also fought to give me, a German child, the chance for a life which was free of the evil of Hitler's hideous dictatorship. And I thank God that they did so.

But your students should learn something of how awful war is when enemy children are caught in the cross-hairs of weapons aimed at their parents. I was very young then, not quite five years old when the war ended in May, 1945, but I remember vivid flashes from those years, flashes that have indelibly etched themselves on my memory.

I was born in Berlin, where we lived until the bombing became extreme and parents were offered the chance for evacuation to less troubled parts of the country. In the case of my mother and me, we went to live in rural Upper Silesia, which now forms part of Poland. My earliest memory of the bombing comes from a moment when I was quite small, when I was awakened in the middle of the night amid thundering noise, and carried to the street. Outside, the air was filled with countless burning embers which fell on us like hail, igniting hair and clothing. My mother ran alongside, swatting my head and clothing and trying to cover me with a shawl.

The raids mounted in frequency, and life became a routine of being awakened, taken from a warm bed, and carried or made to stumble into the air raid shelter. Night after night, with the accompanying music of wailing sirens and the weird physics of air responding to high explosives. The shelters were damp and cold and smelled of dust, tobacco smoke, and sweat. Dust invaded the cramped spaces from being shaken loose by the bombing. It was a smell that lingers, even now. In my Godmother's apartment one night, I stood at the window watching as thousands (I guess) of search lights probed the sky for Allied planes. It was a fascinating thing to see. The bomb impact zone seemed far away, but the pressure was nonetheless enough to implode the window and glass disintegrated around me like a confetti shower.

I got to be very good at taking apart and fitting the canister gas masks with which all air raid shelters were supplied. People used to warn me, "you'll break the glass and cut your finger."

Near the end of the war, in the spring of 1945, I used to stretch out on my back on a grassy field and watch by the hour as those Air Corps bombers flew overhead. These were the 1,000 bomber raids headed for Berlin and the industrial parts of the country. This was in Elend, a village in the Harz Mountains of north-central Germany. Those bombers filled the sky, row upon row, hour after hour, roaring overhead. Eventually, they came almost non-stop day and night. I woke up screaming every night for many years after the show was over.

Sudden noises or lights at night bring me up rigid, heart pumping...and I am 53. At age 21, I was in Vietnam as a U.S. Army advisor when we came under our first mortar attack. It sounds not unlike an oncoming express train. Actually, I was is the bathroom. "OK," I told myself, "you've heard all this before. Don't get overextended. Easy. You're a pro at this." I didn't rush, lit a cigarette, took a drag...and put the thing into my mouth backwards. So much for being an unruffled pro!

We were in the basement of the house in Elend when the American Army came. All houses had to fly a white flag, and I helped our landlord put flags up at each window. That night we heard more battling and in the early morning hours came the first real silence. I think the silence woke me up. Americans were running from house to house and we heard our front door open, above, and footsteps came to the basement trapdoor. With us were a number of wounded German troops and my mother who served as a field nurse. These soldiers clustered themselves around the foot of the stairs. It was, I learned later, because the Americans might throw a grenade.

The GI came down the steps very, very slowly. Half way down he saw the glint of German uniforms and when he suddenly stopped, my mother panicked. She held up the sleeve of one of the Germans, pointed to the insignia and screamed over and over, "Doktor! Doktor! Doktor!" The GI nodded and motioned us all outside, with our hands on top of our heads. All of us stood in a row with our backs to the house, hands on heads, and watched as the soldiers, their jeeps and their tanks occupied the village. And so it was I glimpsed my first Americans.

Later, when we were told that the Russians were coming to take the village, my mother and I joined the columns of refugees heading west. I helped push the baby carriage loaded with what we had in the way of possessions. Berlin was unrecognizable as a city. The bombings razed vast acres and houses had collapsed across streets so nothing was familiar. There was no water, no electric light, no fuel, no money (all the Hitler-era money no longer worked), and very little food. There was no school, no street signs, no restaurants, no shops, no clothing except what we had on our backs, and what we could find. For a time, we lived inside the stone front door of a bombed out house, under three sheets of corrugated steel—part of a Quonset hut.

My mother did inventive stuff like trade cigarette lighter flints and matches for food. Since none of these things was being manufactured any longer, the economy was all by barter. I became some-what expert in scrounging from Allied soldiers, especially Americans who seemed as rich as kings. I could follow and nag a GI until he would either duck completely out of sight or yield. Cigarettes and food were the chief goals. If I got a whole, unsmoked cigarette we actually had enough in trade for a cou-ple of meals. If all I got was a partially smoked butt, my mother would save the tobacco until she had enough to roll a complete "used" cigarette—which was not worth quite as much.

Competition for these treasures was grim and merciless. The most dangerous opposition came from kids who had lost their legs, boys and girls. These children wrapped their stumps in rags and moved about on boards, low to the ground, equipped with wheels. They propelled themselves with their arms and they were lightning fast and completely unsentimental, using the boards as rams. One of my finest prizes was finding a Knights' Cross, Germany's highest decoration, but one of the amputees also saw it at about the same time and we both went for it. The boy had no legs, and his fingers were also gone. He let me examine his hands, and it looked as if the fingers had melted into the palms. Anyhow, his clubbed fists failed to pick up the metal and I got it. But he was older than I was, and managed to talk me into trading. These amputees could, and did, break the legs of those not swift enough to dart in and out of their maneuverings.

I regularly got lice. We all did, and one of the scariest experiences was provided gratis by the U.S. Army who rounded us up in rows and stuck huge syringes full of DDT powder down our backs and fronts. It was the dramatic puff of powder that scared me most.

In 1947, my mother married an Englishman, a member of the Royal Air Force in Germany on occupation service, and I got a new name and grew up in Wales and England. At the age of 17, in 1958, unaccompanied I emigrated to the United States making the transit aboard the freighter *SS Zoella Lykes*, landing in the port of Mobile, Alabama. I earned my passage by dropping out of school and working in the Gloucester, England dockyards. I have never looked back. I have spent over 30 years in uniform, active duty and reserve, and hold the grade of commander in the U.S. Navy. My six real American children have grown up to be fine, talented, kindly people.

Perhaps your students will understand from this brief account that war is the most terrible sin to befall humankind, and that even when war is necessary because the evil is so great, the suffering and the ruin is a horror of indescribable dimension.

With every good wish,
Eric J. Berryman
Formerly Erik Juergen-Karl Dietrich

October 1993

Commander Berryman's letter was delayed in the mail so Gail did not respond until October 13, 1993.

Dear CMDR Berryman, USNR

Your letter of 3 September arrived at Mark Twain School last week. I was so happy to hear from you. I had regretted not obtaining your name and address when we spoke on the phone.

I have been keeping the principal informed about the developments in our fifth-grade project. She, in turn, keeps the superintendent informed. Dr. Cleary has supported our project from the very beginning. I'm sure being a Colonel in the Army Reserves increases his interest in this phase of American history. Last Friday, he sought me out at a district-wide meeting to say how wonderful it was that you took the time to write your letter to our students.

The *World War II Dispatch* article about our school project mentioned the award we won through the A&E Cable Network. The year before, we also won an award using documentary film footage from the Discovery Channel. This year, I plan to use a five-part series offered through A&E Classroom, starting in January. The program, to be shown on Monday mornings, is entitled "The Germans in World War II." After the students see the programs, I plan to share your letter and photographs with them. If you would be willing, I'm sure several students would want to correspond with you.

Our superintendent even wondered if it would be possible for you to visit our school in the spring. We always do a year-end program, "Fifth Graders Focus on the Forties" for the parents. In the past, we have scheduled this program just before Memorial Day. If you thought a visit would be possible, our students could try raising money to at least cover your hotel expenses. You would be our very special Guest of Honor.

I thank you for writing to us and hope you will consider a greater involvement with our project. If you'll call or write a brief note about the possibility of coming to Mark Twain School, I'll be able to start making arrangements for a fund-raiser. However, I won't tell the students about our plans. Instead, I'll let them invite you after we read and discuss your letter and experiences.

I hope we'll have the chance to meet you in person!

Sincerely,
Gail Elliott Thomas, Librarian

The following week, Commander Berryman wrote:

Dear Gail—

I am delighted with your invitation and only too pleased to accept. Enclosed is a <u>vitae</u> for any use you may have for it. By all means give your students the opportunity to share their thoughts and questions with me.

With warm regards,
Eric

After receiving a positive response from Eric Berryman, Gail notified her principal and the superintendent of the school district. As the school year progressed, the fifth graders would study Germany and how the war affected the civilians, children included. The students would also personally invite Commander Berryman to visit St. Louis and would participate in fund-raising efforts to help with his expenses.

Early November 1993

The second intriguing phone call, also generated by the article in the *World War II Dispatch* occurred in early November. It was from June Wandrey Mann, a World War II Army nurse who lived in Kalamazoo, Michigan. [*Editor's note:* June was the second World War II veteran from Kalamazoo, with ties to George's 456th Bomb Group, that Gail had the pleasure of meeting when she spent time in that city visiting family.] Former Lieutenant Wandrey had been the guest speaker at a World War II Commemorative Community event in Louisiana and saw the article about the Black Suitcase in a copy of the *World War II Dispatch*. She wondered if Gail would like a copy of her book, *Bedpan Commando* for the school library. *(Fig. 51)*

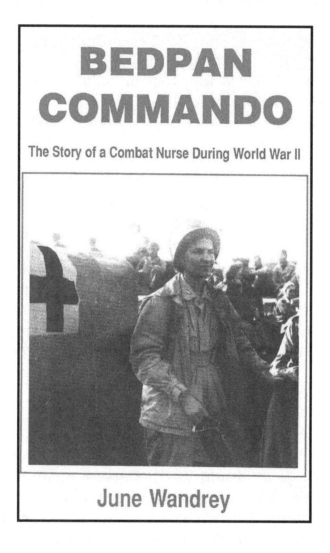

Figure 51: Lt. June Wandrey, U.S. Army Nurse Corps pictured in front of a field hospital somewhere in Europe during World War II

As mentioned before, the fifth-grade World War II project had a few critics and one of them was Gail's own mother who wondered when women would be in the story. Perhaps *Bedpan Commando* would reveal an association.

The following week, June Wandrey mailed her book to Gail. June's letter, written on November 8, 1993 began:

> Dear Gail,
>
> Award-winning Librarian! Commemorative Community project innovator. Because of you... eager 5th graders are sopping up World War II history and loving the thrill of the chase. You must glow even in the daylight. Call me when you come to Kalamazoo again. Wandrey is my maiden name.
>
> Yes, I discovered you in the *World War II Dispatch* that was given to me when I participated in the Slidell, LA Commemorative Community affair September 23-24-25. On the 24th I gave my *Bedpan Commando* book review.

With her book, June included copies of two book reviews. One review had comments made by Paul Harvey:

> Laughingly labeled a Bedpan Commando by the troops, June Wandrey recorded World War II from ambulance and tent as her mobile surgical unit followed the infantry.
>
> *Bedpan Commando* is a nurse's story of a man's war from Fort Custer [Michigan] to Dachau [Germany] and all the bloody spots in between. Across North Africa and on to Sicily, Italy, France, Germany,

Allach and Dachau, these women fought death, despair, and exhaustion with humor, tears and guts.

From diary and letters and illustrated with 20 pages of never-before-published photographs, *Bedpan Commando* chronicles Wandrey's coming-of-age while the world learned to capitalize the word Holocaust. Hysterical, historical, funny and sad.

The second review was written by Brigadier General Connie Slewitzke, USA NC (Ret.) Vice President, WIMSA and former Chief, Army Nurse Corps.

Bedpan Commando by June Wandrey.

The title of this book can never describe the caring, competence and professionalism of this courageous Army surgical nurse. Through her letters home, notes and diary, we participate in the campaigns of North Africa, Sicily, Italy, France and Germany. Everyone who reads Ms. Wandrey's harrowing accounts of combat nursing will identify with the heroism and dedication of this outstanding soldier. Ms. Wandrey captivates our interests as she describes the extremely rudimentary living conditions, inhospitable climate and the constant stress of coping with mass casualties, enemy air raids and shellings, often while very ill herself. We come to know personalities, some never to be forgotten, who add to the misery of war. We identify with her as she comforts the wounded, grieves for the dying and weeps because of man's inhumanity to man. Above all, we learn June Wandrey is a survivor. She met every challenge with a professionalism that stands out as a shining example for today's military women to emulate.

June Wandrey and other nurses arrived home without fanfare. They disembarked at a deserted pier at Newport News, Virginia. The final irony was a ride on a filthy, insect infested train. That's how a country welcomed home women of great courage and honor following World War II. Women who gave so much, yet received little or no appreciation or recognition for their service, even to this day. This book should be recommended reading for today's military women.

When June's book arrived at school, Gail had to set it aside for later reading because the students were preparing for their Veterans Day program which was to be held on November 10, 1993. They were introduced to the Tuskegee Airmen by listening to Mrs. Kalyn Brantley-McNeal tell about her father's experiences in World War II. The late Major Charles Brantley had an illustrious career which included forty-two missions and ten awards and medals, among them the Distinguished Flying Cross. His granddaughter was a member of the current fifth-grade class and introduced the guest speaker for the Veterans Day program.

World War II pilot Christopher Newman, member of the 332nd Fighter Group known as the "Fighting Red Tails" spoke before the students and guests which included the school district's superintendent and the town's mayor. Mr. Newman was a member of the Tuskegee Airmen and the Caterpillar Club. Membership in the Caterpillar Club is limited to those who had parachuted from flaming aircraft. *(Fig. 52)*

The local cable television company taped the presentation and showed the entire hour-long program several times on November 11th throughout the St. Louis metropolitan area. When thanking Mr. Newman, School Superintendent Dr. John Cleary commented, "We were riveted to our chairs. It is an honor to be in the presence of American heroes."

Figure 52: Tuskegee Airmen and St. Louis resident Chris Newman speaking to Mark Twain fifth-grade students in honor of Veterans Day 1993

Later that month, Dr. Cleary paid tribute to Mr. Newman during the November School Board Meeting and Gail was able to present the records of the 332nd Fighter Group to Mr. Newman. She had obtained the declassified war material while visiting the Air Force Historical Research Center in Montgomery, Alabama the previous July.

Late November 1993

After the Veterans Day activities were completed, Gail continued reading *Bedpan Commando* and wrote the following on November 30, 1993:

Dear June,

Your book and nice note arrived two weeks ago... your book sounds just like your letter! I'm so glad you discovered Mark Twain's fifth-grade project through the *World War II Dispatch*. Did you know that your story has a direct connection with ours? I could hardly believe my eyes when I read page 122 in your book: your 7-15-44 trip to visit "Mike" brought you to the 456th Bomb Group with Col. Steed as its commander. I think you mention "Mike" only once…was he special to you? What is his name and when did you see him last? Is he still living?

You probably feel as I do, sometimes, when reflecting on the developments that have occurred with both of our projects. Who would have imagined so many different experiences could come from a bunch of old letters?

Sure hope I have a chance to meet you in December! Please tell me more about "Mike."

Gail's questions about "Mike" were generated by three entries in June's book:

7-13-44 Somewhere in Italy
Dear Betty,

Mother said Mike is near Foggia in the Air Force. As soon as I can hitchhike to an airport and find a plane going that way, I'll go and visit him.

7-15-44 Flew to Foggia in a B-25 to see Mike at Cerignola. Spent the night with my toothbrush at the 34th Field Hospital and saw three nurse friends from Custer.

7-17-44 Italy
Dear Betty,

Mike went on a bombing mission at 3 AM over the Ploesti oil fields in Romania. I wanted to go along, but they were afraid to take me because no one knew I was here. If we got shot down and survived, what would happen to me. When the mission returned, one plane was on fire and most of the men bailed out just short of the field. One airman's parachute didn't open. Everyone was screaming, "Pull the cord, pull the cord." The pilot landed the plane safely. Mike was ashen as he got out of his plane. A dud had gone between his legs and lodged in the canopy above his head.

Much later that day, Mike and Jim flew me in a B-24 Liberator to Pomigliano as I had no other way to get back to where we were bivouacking. As they had no reason to be in that area they told me they would just do a rolling touch-down and I should jump out of the plane, duck, and run as fast as I could to the edge of the airport and disappear in the brush. I did as instructed, barely touching ground in my race. Working my way back to the road, I got a ride with a man from ordnance. He thought my jump and run exercise sounded exciting. I asked to be let off about half-a-mile from camp and nonchalantly walked the rest of the way, just in time for the confusion of chow-time. Love June

General Nathan Twining was the Commanding General of the 15ᵗʰ Air Force. Five hundred planes went on the raid, ten men in each plane. Mike's group of between 36-40 planes, under the command of Colonel Steed, were known as the Flying Horses. Their target was the Amerino Romano oil refineries.

The flak was heavy, intense and accurate. On the return trip, they were attacked by 12 ME 109s.

June wrote that Mike's bomb group… "under the command of Colonel Steed were known as the Flying Horses." She was almost correct. Colonel Steed's bomb group were known as the "Flying Colts," not the "Flying Horses," and George Elliott Rich was a member of that same bomb group! *(Fig. 53)* [*Editor's note:* This is another coincidence in the Black Suitcase Mystery.] Gail now had the direct connection needed to include the Army Nurse Corps in the story. Her mother was delighted!

On December 7, 1993 June wrote and answered some of Gail's questions about "Mike."

456th BOMB GROUP (H) WWII

304th BOMB WING

15th AIR FORCE

"Steed's Flying Colts"

OVERSEAS MILITARY CEMETERIES

A listing of members interred in overseas cemeteries, those returned to the USA for re-burial, and all other known deceased members of the 456th Bomb Group.

Figure 53: The 456th Bomb Group, which included George Elliott Rich, was known as "Steed's Flying Colts"

Dear Gail,

Great hearing from you.

"Mike" is Myron Koechel a bomber pilot. My father and his father were cousins 2nd or 3rd maybe. As my father was nearly 50 when I was born, my 1st cousins were old enough to be my parents. I graduated from high school in 1937 when I was 16. According to the 1990 Alumni Directory, Mike graduated in 1939. He still lives in Wautoma, Wisconsin. I saw him briefly in 1990 at the OVER FIFTY Wautoma High School Reunion. His wife died many years ago and he had not remarried.

The pilot on my fright-flight back to Pomigliano was Jim Gardner from Texas. He died a few years ago. I've regretted not including the story about the trip to the 34th hospital for the night. Jim drove the jeep, Mike and I sat in the back seat. It was a gorgeous night. I'm a chatty person and the soldiers always appreciated having an American woman to talk to so I was doing my best. Finally Jim turned to us and said, "Hey Mike, what's your problem you're on one side of the jeep and June's on the other?" Mike was very shy and didn't answer. I said, 'We're cousins." Jim stopped the jeep and said, "Let's trade places, you drive." Just then we arrived at the 34th.

November 29th I had outpatient exploratory surgery. December 22nd (the earliest date we could get) I'm having majorish surgery. Should still be in the Bronson Hospital on the 26th. It would be a pleasure to meet you and your husband there. If I've been discharged I demand that you come to our home.

There'll be no dancing allowed and I'll give up my three mile daily hike for a while.

Gail and June met, at her home, on December 26, 1993 and began a correspondence which lasted many years. June continued to take an active interest in the fifth graders' project and made two trips to St. Louis before the commemoration period ended in 1995.

THIRD YEAR OF THE PROJECT:
School Year 1993-1994, Second Semester

January 1994

When school resumed after the holidays, *A&E Classroom* began showing the documentary film footage about life in Germany during World War II. Gail taped the episodes and showed them to the fifth graders. She also shared the letter that Navy Commander Eric Berryman had written earlier in the year.

February 1994

The students were captivated by Commander Berryman's letter. It was a sobering experience to read how different his childhood experiences were compared to theirs. They wrote a letter to him on February 9, 1994:

Dear Commander Berryman,

We are the fifth graders of Mark Twain School. We know about you because you wrote a letter to Mrs. Thomas and we read it. You know about us because of the *World War II Dispatch* article. We think it would be nice if you could meet us and we could meet you.

We have seen a show on *A&E Classroom* about Germans in World War II. We watched the video about German cities being bombed and realized how sad it was. We saw where your home town of Berlin was bombed.

We want to invite you to come to our school in May, just before Memorial Day Weekend, to tell us more about your childhood during World War II. We would really like to meet you. Both classes would. Commander Berryman, if you could come and visit us, we will raise money for some of the expenses of your trip.

We have a lot of pictures for you to see and we have medals, too. Do you have any medals for us to see? We could share with you the information that we have learned. We could also pass it to other people who are interested in World War II by asking Continental Cablevision and the newspapers to cover your visit.

If you can come to see St. Louis, besides visiting Mark Twain School, here are places you can see: The Arch, The Science Center, The Missouri Botanical Garden and The Art Museum.

Hope you can make it!
Sincerely,
The Fifth Graders of Mark Twain School

March 1994

On March 3, 1994 Commander Berryman responded to the students' invitation:

Dear Children:

I am happy to accept your kind invitation to come and meet you and to talk about my experiences as a small boy in war-time Germany. Ms. Thomas says I should plan on being with you May 26 and 27 and that I may bring my two nieces, Karen and Sara Truckey, who live in nearby Alton, Illinois. Memorial Day, which honors our Civil War dead, is a good time to think about all wars.

You ask about medals. Well, the only 1939-45 medals I have to show you belong to my step-father, John Berryman, who served in England's Royal Air Force all through World War II, and the combat patrol badges awarded to my uncle, Guenther Jahrisch, for his participation as a petty-officer crewman in the German Navy's U-Boat arm, 1938-45. Besides these, I have my own awards from more than 30 years in American uniform, including service as an Advisor to the Army of the Republic of Viet Nam, in country, during the early stages of the war, 1962-63. I will bring all the medals for you to examine and discuss.

Again, thank you so much for asking me to meet you, and thank you also for trying to raise some of the expenses of the trip. I look forward to seeing your faces and being in your company.

With every good wish,
Yours sincerely,
Eric J. Berryman
Commander, USNR

April 1994

Throughout the years of the school project, the students were fortunate to have the help of Mr. Lee Reisenleiter, a Brentwood resident, who had served with the 82nd Airborne Division during World War II. He was a tremendous asset as the 50th Anniversary of D-Day approached. The night of June 5, 1944 Mr. Reisenleiter and hundreds of other soldiers parachuted behind enemy lines into France in advance of the June 6th invasion. He shared his experiences with the fifth graders as they began their research projects and the *St. Louis Post Dispatch* published the following about his visit to Mark Twain School.

> "World War II Veteran Opens Students' Eyes: 5th Graders See Shrapnel, Equipment, Get Glimpse of D-Day, Battle of Bulge"
> by Carolyn Bower of the *Post-Dispatch* staff
>
> When veteran Lee Reisenleiter jumped from a C-47 plane over France 50 years ago, he dodged German bullets and landed with a parachute full of holes.
>
> "You look out in the dark and see cherry dots from the gunfire," Reisenleiter told a rapt audience of fifth graders at Mark Twain Elementary School in Brentwood. "The flak hits the plane and you feel it rock. You have to swallow a couple times before you step out."
>
> Reisenleiter, 72, won two purple hearts and scores of ribbons and awards for his service as an Army paratrooper and explosives expert in World War II. He was 20 at the time.
>
> For the last three years, he has visited Mark Twain to talk about his experiences as a veteran of the 82nd

Airborne Division in D-Day and the Battle of the Bulge. This year marks the 50th anniversary of both events.

Reisenleiter began coming to Mark Twain at the invitation of the librarian, Gail Elliott Thomas. She has won numerous awards for bringing veterans and students together to study the World War II era.

Last Wednesday, Reisenleiter came attired in a steel helmet and tan uniform with pockets of show 'n' tell paraphernalia. *(Fig. 54)* He explained that fully dressed with military equipment his weight rose to 300 pounds from 150 pounds.

He passed around a 5-inch lug of shrapnel. He talked about the shrapnel he got in his arm and face. He clicked once on a toy brass cricket to show students how soldiers signaled to one another in battle.

Figure 54: Steel-helmeted WWII veteran Lee Reisenleiter speaking before a group of fifth graders

One by one, he raised a German knife, a flask-size German gun cleaning kit and his pull to a parachute.

He spoke of rifles, bazookas and mortars, and generals such as Montgomery and Patton. He talked about one war job: tracking and tallying dead soldiers.

He showed a group photo of his 508th Parachute Regiment with 147 members before the group went overseas in World War II. At the end of the war after transfers, deaths and injuries, only six remained.

Reisenleiter said he speaks at schools because he wants students to get an idea of the World War II era. It was the one time in his seven decades of living, Reisenleiter says, that people pulled together. The one common objective: the war effort.

Of his student audiences Reisenleiter said: "Children have open minds. If you can sow the seeds of unity, camaraderie and patriotism now, it might make a difference when they are older".

May 1994

As the Memorial Day weekend approached, plans were finalized for Commander Berryman's visit. During an assembly, he told the fifth graders about his war-time childhood, living and surviving the bomber attacks in Berlin. It was a sobering presentation. *(Fig. 55)* Afterwards, he spent time with the students, helping with their final display preparations and talking with them in small groups.

The D-Day commemoration became larger than anyone could have imagined. As mentioned before, Mark Twain School was the *first* elementary school in the United States to be designated as a World War II Commemorative Community.

Figure 55: U.S. Navy Commander Eric Berryman during his visit to Mark Twain Elementary School May 1994

Mark Twain School was unique because fifth graders were doing the commemoration events, not high school students or adults.

Whenever a major World War II anniversary approached, the national news media contacted the Department of Defense World War II Commemoration Committee's Public Relations and Education officer and asked, "What's happening in the schools?" Major Phyllis Phipps-Barnes would always suggest that they, "Check out what's happening at Mark Twain Elementary School in Brentwood, Missouri."

At the local level, St. Louis-affiliated stations from the three major networks sent camera crews and reporters to Mark Twain School to film the Memorial Day program. They interviewed Lee Reisenleiter, paratroop veteran of the D-Day invasion, and filmed the various student projects and displays. It was a busy and exciting event for all involved. *(Fig. 56)*

The highlight for the students, however, was riding in *Thumper* a World War II half-track on the school's grass field. *(Fig. 57)*

At the national level, a reporter and photographer from *USA Today* documented the school's D-Day observance. The article and two colored photos appeared in the June 1, 1994 edition of the paper with the headline "Tactical Approaches to Teaching D-Day, Learning Appreciation from World War II Lessons". *(Fig. 58)*

Mark Twain principal, Jackie Whitworth, shared her thoughts in the article:

> Teaching about World War II is a good way to bring together senior citizens and elementary students. Intergenerational study is something all our staff is interested in. It gets them talking to their neighbors and appreciating what people did for our country 50 years ago.

Figure 56: D-Day veteran Lee Reisenleiter being interviewed by television reporters May 1994

Figure 57: Students enjoying a ride in *Thumper* a WWII vintage half-track May 1994

Figure 58: Article in *USA TODAY* about Mark Twain Elementary School's 50th anniversary observance of D-Day June 1994

An even greater honor had occurred two days earlier. President William Clinton, in his Memorial Day speech at Arlington National Cemetery, May 30, 1994 cited the Mark Twain Elementary School's World War II project! What a way to end the school year!

The *Weekly Compilation of Presidential Documents*, published every Monday by the Office of the Federal Register, National Archives and Records Administration, contains statements, messages, and other Presidential materials released by the White House during the preceding week. The comments below, printed on page 1187 of the *Weekly Compilation of Presidential Documents* and published on Monday, June 6, 1994, were part of the "Remarks at a Memorial Day Ceremony in Arlington, Virginia" on May 30, 1994. President Clinton had made reference to the 50th anniversary of the World War II campaign at Normandy and in Italy.

> Learning about those times and deeds must be more than accidental. Fortunately, many of our fellow Americans understand that. Gail Thomas of Brentwood Missouri, was one of them. Her parents both served in World War II. She's a librarian at the Mark Twain Elementary School in her community and every year she brings in veterans of D-Day and other battles to speak to the students. She says the kids can't believe what those gray-haired men did when they were young. Then they understand that America is the way it is today because of what people gave up 50 years ago.

June 1994

The Saturday, June 4, 1994 issue of the *St. Louis Post Dispatch* included a special page devoted to the "D-Day: 50th Anniversary" and included an article entitled "Librarian's Black Valise Helps Pupils Live World War II" written by Carolyn Bower.

When veterans flock to Normandy on Monday to remember the 50th anniversary of D-Day, a librarian from Brentwood will join their ranks. *(Fig. 59)*

The librarian, Gail Elliott Thomas, plans to visit Ste. Mere Eglise on Sunday and Utah Beach and the American Cemetery at Colleville-sur-Mer on Monday.

For Thomas, 47, the trip is the latest step in a historical adventure that brought her recognition from President Bill Clinton in a Memorial Day speech at Arlington National Cemetery.

Clinton mentioned that Thomas had brought together veterans and elementary pupils at Mark Twain School in Brentwood.

Figure 59: President Bill Clinton with WWII D-Day veterans on Normandy Beach, France June 6, 1994

For three years Thomas has used a black suitcase to entice her fifth graders to learn more about World War II. The suitcase contains letters from George Elliott Rich, the cousin of Thomas' father. The children studied news accounts of his plane, a B-24 bomber. They read about his death at age 22 in 1944 on his 50th mission.

From veterans, children have heard firsthand of the Allied invasion of Europe. They learned that Operation Overlord was the secret name for the offensive June 6, the storming of the French coast that marked the beginning of World War II's end.

Some pupils have researched their own family histories during World War II. Others have studied battles or the home front and experiences of people involved.

One pupil told Thomas he felt like he was living a novel, quite a compliment for a librarian.

When Gail returned home from Normandy, she found a letter written by Commander Berryman. He had written a thank you letter on June 3, 1994 and had high praise for the World War II commemoration events he had seen at Mark Twain School.

Dear Gail:

Many, many thanks for your kindnesses and care during my visit with you. The trip, your students, Mark Twain School and the wonderful people I was privileged to meet have enriched my life – and also made a lasting impression on my niece, Karen. Your project to commemorate World War II is quite likely unrivalled by any similar school effort in the entire country. I am proud to have played a small role in the Grand Finale for the school year—illuminated by music and spiced with tooth-picked spam.

I look forward to hearing of your continuing successes, and perhaps we can collaborate some more viz a viz [*sic*] fundraising for the Liberator visit next year.

There is no need to ask whether your visit to Normandy was memorable or not. You shared in a great event, as bitter-sweet and as historically important and unique as any there ever was. I hope you brought back of handful of sand from one or another of the beaches where the light of day was extinguished for so many gallant young men, long ago.

With every good wish,
Eric

FOURTH YEAR OF THE PROJECT:
School Year 1994-1995, First Semester

September 1994
When the new school year began, the educators realized the next major event on the World War II anniversary calendar would be the National and International 50th Anniversary Observance of the Battle of the Bulge. Another coincidence: the reunion and ceremonies would be held in St. Louis, Missouri! *(Fig. 60)*

The Mark Twain fifth-grade students received an official invitation to participate in the Battle of the Bulge Parade and

Plaque Dedication Ceremony scheduled for December 16, 1994. They were to join the U.S. Army Band and 25 Trumpeters from the Belgium Guides Band who were traveling with their Ambassador.

Gail knew that World War II Army Nurse June Wandrey Mann had seen action in the Battle of the Bulge and told the latest group of fifth graders about her. On September 6, 1994 they wrote to June.

Figure 60: Newsletter announcing the 50th Anniversary of the Battle of the Bulge Commemoration to be held in St. Louis, Missouri

Dear Nurse Wandrey,

Our library teacher is Mrs. Gail Elliott Thomas and her relative was George Elliott Rich. He was in the same B-24 bomb group that your cousin Mike was in. We read in your book *Bedpan Commando* how you made a visit to them in Italy when no one knew you were gone from your hospital.

Our fifth-grade class is studying World War II. We would like you to come and visit us at Mark Twain Elementary School in Brentwood, Missouri, a suburb of St. Louis. We would like you to tell us about World War II. If you do come, please bring your scrapbook and other memorabilia. We will pay for your hotel room and give you refreshments if you are able to come.

We know you were in the Battle of the Bulge. Do you know about the big parade that will be in St. Louis on December 16, 1994? We are going to march in it because Mark Twain Elementary School is very special. We were the first elementary school to be a World War II Commemorative Community.

We will march in the parade with the Veterans of the Battle of the Bulge. If you are not able to march in the parade, we can offer you a ride in a World War II Army half-track. Mr. Tony Petruso, owner of "Overlord Military Collectables" in St. Louis has helped with our school project. He has an Army half-track and will give you a ride.

Please write us back as soon as possible with your answer.

Your admirers,
The Fifth Graders of Mark Twain School

June answered back on September 12, 1994:

Dear Students,

Your gracious invitation arrived yesterday and deserves a *YES* answer. Portage is also a suburb like Brentwood. When my pitching arm is up to snuff, on a good day I can throw a snowball and hit Kalamazoo. Did you ever hear that famous World War II song, "I've Got a Gal in Kalamazoo"?

Yes, I will bring my World War II memorabilia. Hope you recognize me, I'll be in my 51-year-old dress uniform and combat boots. If I get to ride in Mr. Petruso's half-track I'll wear my fatigues and wool underwear with the button fly.

My antique *Stars & Stripes* newspapers will interest you, most are from ETO (European Theater of Operations). A few are from the Pacific theatre.

Fondly,
June Wandrey, the Bedpan Commando

June included a personal letter to Gail with details about how she usually handled her presentations:

Dear Gail,

Tucking in a note for you too.

Please let me know just what approach you want me to use with the 5th graders. Did you want me to speak on a specific facet of the war? My book review is about 35 minutes long. 40 minutes if I give tales from my growing up years. So many people wanted to know how I grew up and had the courage to volunteer to go to war. The review is very funny in spots as it wends its way to getting serious. They'll never forget it.

How many students will there be at this meeting?

I have many pictures that will fascinate them. People spend hours reading the old newspapers. Young folks like to hold the spy camera, etc. and ask me gobs of questions. They can ask me anything.

It's exciting just thinking about being there with you and your bright band of open minds.

For my displays I'll need at least two 8 foot tables. That will permit many children to look at things without standing in line.

If I give my review—I need a podium with a light and a microphone and a glass of water.

Thanks for asking me,
Always,
June

October 1994

The current class of fifth graders did not meet World War II veteran Lee Reisenleiter until early October. A staff writer for the *Mid-County Journal*, Mike Knopfel, wrote an article which his paper published on October 9, 1994:

Brought to Life: World War II History Continues to Unfold at Brentwood School

The fifth-grade students at Mark Twain Elementary School in Brentwood will have history brought to life Wednesday when World War II veteran Lee Reisenleiter shares his experiences of the war.

Reisenleiter, a longtime Brentwood resident, was a veteran of D-Day and the Battle of the Bulge. He'll speak to students at 9 a.m. in the library at the school.

Reisenleiter's visit will be the first of three Battle of the Bulge events coming up for the Mark Twain students. On December 15, World War II nurse June Wandrey will speak to the fifth graders. Wandrey is the recipient of eight battle stars (now called service stars) and also was involved in the Battle of the Bulge.

The students learned about Wandrey from her book *Bedpan Commando*. Wandrey lives in Michigan. The students raised money to pay for her lodging while she is here.

The Mark Twain students will also participate in the 50th Anniversary Parade for the Battle of the Bulge Commemoration on Dec. 16 in downtown St. Louis.

Thomas said Reisenleiter will wear a replica of his paratrooper uniform during his presentation. She said having a veteran talk with the students will give them a personal view of the war and its consequences.

"The war changed everybody," Thomas said. "Mr. Reisenleiter was slated to be a Dodger's baseball player. Then the war came. It really did change his whole future."

"The kids marvel at that," Thomas said. "Here's this gray-haired veteran who could have been playing baseball with the Dodgers."

Mr. Reisenleiter captivated the attention of one fifth-grader who said, "His story was just really interesting. He's just so brave, I don't know how anybody could do that. Plus he was our first speaker and kind of brought us into everything."

December 1994

The first two weeks of December were spent getting everything ready for the Battle of the Bulge activities and June Wandrey's visit. June arrived in St. Louis on December 14th and spoke to the fifth graders the next day. *(Fig. 61)*

The audience for June's presentation included the mayor of Brentwood, World War II veteran Mr. Lee Reisenleiter and other local citizens who had helped with the four-year project.

Resolutions recognizing the program were presented by both the Missouri House of Representatives and the Missouri Senate. Officials from Continental Cable honored Gail for her use of cable programming and Nicholas Davatzes, president and CEO of the Arts and Entertainment cable network, sent a video message of congratulations to the students at Mark Twain.

Figure 61: Battle of the Bulge veteran, WWII Army Nurse Lt. June Wandrey speaking before Mark Twain fifth-grade students December 15, 1994

Newspaper reporters from the *St. Louis Post Dispatch* and the *Mid-County Journal* listened to June's presentation. Continental Cablevision filmed the event for broadcast in the greater St. Louis metropolitan area.

A special correspondent from the *St. Louis Post Dispatch*, Linda Jarrett, wrote:

> World War II Army Nurse Recalls 'Bedpan Commando' Life
>
> Standing in her Army nursing uniform, complete with combat boots, retired 1st Lt. June Wandrey recently told fifth graders at Mark Twain Elementary School in Brentwood, "Here you have a 50-year-old uniform with a 74-year-old body inside."
>
> Fresh out of nursing school, Wandrey was listening to the radio and dreaming of medical school on

Dec. 7, 1941, when President Franklin D. Roosevelt interrupted and announced the bombing of Pearl Harbor.

She and a friend promptly tried to enlist, but they were 21 years old, and they had to be 22. After Wandrey's birthday in February, she joined the Army Nurse Corps. "The army gave us no training in combat, regulations, marching, anything, but we volunteered to go to North Africa when the Army landed."

"We were like little field mice following the 45th Infantry Division from battle to battle," Wandrey said. "From North Africa, we went to Sicily, then to Anzio Beachhead where we were surrounded by the Germans."

Wandrey said they had heard Hitler was going to attack the Allies in the Ardennes Forest in Belgium and Luxembourg and drive through to Antwerp. The Germans began the push on Dec. 16, 1944.

The Battle of the Bulge was fought in an abundance of snow, ice and slush in frigid conditions, Wandrey said. "Over one million men were involved from the United States, Britain, Belgium, Canada, and France. We had 81,000 casualties with 19,000 killed."

Wandrey said that when most people think of hospitals, "They think of long corridors, starched uniforms, things squeaky clean. We worked in field tents."

Wandrey described her Christmas in 1944. "We sterilized our equipment and set up a hospital in an old bombed-out factory. We put up a little tree, decorated it with tinsel and wrapping paper from packages from home and were even going to have some turkey, when a soldier burst in and said our troops had been overrun, and we had to leave."

Wandrey said they had no transportation and had to wait for the quartermaster to come with trucks. "We were hoping he'd get there before the Germans". Gradually, the Allies pushed the German 'bulge' back, and our field hospital followed the 45th all over Germany."

"I started keeping a diary, but some of the things were too bad to write about," Wandrey said. "We had many gruesome days and nights."

This summer, Wandrey returned to Anzio Beachhead in Italy for the D-Day Commemoration at Anzio-Nettuno Cemetery, where she met President Clinton. "He never took his eyes off me while we were talking," Wandrey recalled, grinning. *(Fig. 62)*

Wandrey said she hadn't planned on writing a book. "But, in 1985, my daughter found all my letters, clippings, pictures, even negatives. After putting them all in chronological order, she sent them to a publisher interested in military work."

"He sent me a hate letter," Wandrey shrugged. "He said everything about the war had been written, and what I had was boring and sophomoric." In 1990, Wandrey self-published *The Bedpan Commando*, which details her 32 months in Europe.

Writing her book was both therapeutic and traumatic for her and for others, Wandrey said. "Last summer I was in Mobile, and a woman came up to me and said, 'My husband died at Anzio Beachhead, and all this time I was angry. Now, I've met you, and I know he didn't die alone.'"

Figure 62: June Wandrey with President Bill Clinton at the 50th Anniversary of the Battle for Anzio observance, Italy June 3, 1994

Mike Knopfel, staff writer for the *Mid-County Journal* contributed additional information:

Students Get Firsthand Account of War

After concluding her talk to fifth-grade students at Mark Twain Elementary School in Brentwood, an emotional June Wandrey Mann stepped back from the podium and snapped off a salute.

The memories of World War II are always with Mann. She was a United States Army combat nurse in Europe for almost three years.

Mann, 74, a resident of Kalamazoo, Mich., was in St. Louis to take part in the 50th anniversary commemoration of the Battle of the Bulge. Since the war, Mann has returned to Europe several times. This past summer she joined President Clinton in a memorial service at the Anzio-Nettuno, Italy cemetery.

Mann wasn't fazed when Pentagon officials asked if she would like to meet the president. "They asked, 'Would you be comfortable talking to the president?'" Mann said, "Of course, I'm old enough to be his mother."

She addressed the Mark Twain students wearing full military dress uniform. Her outfit also included combat boots and support hose.

"The hose came in handy," Mann said. "When you're a combat nurse, you have to stand up to 12 to 20 hours. Your veins start to give out after a while, so you have to wear support hose. If a soldier is wounded, he gets a Purple Heart, but if you're injured, you just get scar tissue."

"The Battle of the Bulge was fought in snow, sleet and ice," Mann said. Mann vividly remembers Christmas night, 1944. Her unit, which was usually quartered in tents, had the luxury of spending the night in a bombed-out factory. "At least it had a roof, but the windows were blown out and there were some holes in the wall," she said. "Just as we were getting comfortable, we were told the Germans had overrun our troops and we would have to go. There we were surrounded by half-cooked turkeys and singing Christmas carols as we waited to move out."

Her unit took refuge in a field. Some people slept in a barn with cows. Throughout the night, the sound of tanks rumbling down a nearby road could be heard. Mann said their identity wouldn't be discovered until morning. "At dawn we saw tanks of the (U.S.) 12th Armored Division," she said. "They had that big, white glorious star on them. It was a beautiful sight."

Before school recessed for the Christmas holidays, each student wrote a thank you note to Nurse Wandrey. On January 3, 1995 June wrote the following letter:

Dear Students,

I enjoyed all thirty-four letters. These are the answers to your many questions.

Did you like our singing to you and did it make you happy?

Your singing "I've Got a Gal in Kalamazoo" made me feel like I was twenty two years old again. No wrinkles.

Did you think you would live through World War II?

Yes. I always wanted to live to be 100 years old so that I could date my letters 2020. That was long before the television show of the same name.

Why did you decide to publish your experiences during World War II as a book? And are you proud of *Bedpan Commando*?

I didn't know until 1985 that my parents, who had died in the 1960s, had saved all most [*sic*] all of my World War II letters and negatives. When I found this shriveled old cardboard box and these historical and hysterical letters, I wanted everyone in the world to know what it really was like being a combat nurse. As I read the letters over I cried and cried, and laughed and laughed. This material was buried so deep in my soul I didn't know it existed. I went back to my old, early post war pattern of not sleeping soundly.

If I did get to sleep after hours of putting the letters on the computer in chronological order, I would wake up because my pillow was soaked with tears and I didn't know that I had been crying.

Yes, I'm proud of my service chronicled in this book.

Would you have rather been with your family on Christmas day 1944?

No. The wounded needed me more than my family did.

Were you ever scared Christmas day?

Too busy that day to be scared. Mostly curious about what would happen next and what I would do if captured.

How many places did you work as a nurse?

During World War II...Fort Custer, Michigan, Africa, Sicily, Italy, France and Germany.

How many decorations did you earn?

Eight battlestars, some meritorious awards, four ribbons, five overseas bars.

I want to ask you how long you were in the service, and were you scared in the service?

I served my country for forty six months. Yes, sometimes.

Where did you work? What did the place that you worked at look like?

Mostly in a tent, usually with a number of flak holes in the top of the canvas. The tent was always in a field. We never knew where we were. The buildings that we were in briefly were always damaged by the war.

How many places were you stationed?

There is nothing stationary about a Field Hospital. As the fighting troops moved we moved behind them.

How many people did you treat each day at the clinic?

We didn't have a clinic. It was a very mobile, primitive hospital. We worked on a 24 hour basis, treating everyone that the ambulances brought to us. The official hospital records would be in the Archives in Washington. The total treated would be in the thousands.

Do you remember the names of the men you treated?

Only one…just his first name. We treated thousands of wounded. In a Field Hospital you move as the Infantry moves. We only kept the soldiers long enough to be strong enough to be moved to the rear hospitals. For our nurses it was another face another place.

Were you a nurse in a bunker or hospital?

In a very mobile tent hospital. We moved so often… do you think it was because we didn't pay the rent on the field we were in?

If you had been so scared and terrified, that you just couldn't go another day living like that, and if you were allowed to go back to America, would you have gone?

No, I wouldn't have gone. When you volunteered for the Army Nurse Corps it was for the duration of the war. I graduated from high school when I was sixteen years old. My graduation speech For Value

Received I Promise To Pay says it all. I owed my country for the privilege of being born here and for the education I had received. When my country was attacked and needed me I paid in full.

WOW! It's midnight and time for me to rest my wrinkles. Any spelling errors you might find in my answers are deliberate.

Fondly,
The Bedpan Commando

After having the experience of meeting and listening to veterans of the Battle of the Bulge, the students had a better understanding of the hardships they faced during that winter-time battle. One fifth-grade girl commented about women during the war:

I just thought they stayed at home, crying and thinking about their sons, husbands or relatives. I have a lot of respect for Nurse Wandrey. She acted really brave.

FOURTH YEAR OF THE PROJECT:
School Year 1994-1995, Second Semester

Once again, the period just before the Christmas holiday recess had been filled with World War II guest speakers and excitement. When school resumed, the current group of students continued with a project their predecessors had initiated in 1993: how to get a World War II era B-24 Liberator Bomber to St. Louis.

Back in 1991, when the Black Suitcase Mystery was first introduced to the fifth graders, no one at Mark Twain Elementary knew much about the B-24 Liberator Bombers. Gail found books, posters, old World War II manuals and diagrams which became valuable resources for the students.

In early 1993, Gail purchased a book and video about the only fully restored B-24, the *All American* owned by the Collings Foundation. The video showed the *All American* making flights across the United States. The students wondered if the B-24 would fly to St. Louis since it was the same type of plane on which their World War II hero, George Elliott Rich, had served.

April 1993

On April 6, 1993 the fifth graders composed a group letter to Mr. Collings:

Dear Mr. Collings,

Hello! We are writing to you from Mark Twain Elementary School in Brentwood, Missouri. Our fifth-grade classes like to learn about past times and we are doing a study/project about World War II.

We are learning about the B-24 Liberator through an award winning project called the "Black Suitcase Mystery." It is about a man named George Elliott Rich who flew in a Liberator called the *Purple Shaft*. He was stationed in Italy and was killed on his 50th mission over Germany in 1944.

We have watched your video about the *All American*. We also have the poster and the book on the *All American*. We know how long and difficult it was to restore the *All American* Liberator and we are <u>very</u> impressed by your actions. We know it took a lot of time and money, but still we appreciate it a lot. We thank you for your hard work.

We would like to know if you would be able to fly the *All American* to St. Louis? We are very interested in seeing a real Liberator. We are going to have a year-end event just before Memorial Day and would love to invite you. We have three airports where you could land. They are: Lambert Field (St. Louis International), Spirit of St. Louis, and Park Bi-State in Illinois.

Please let us know if it is possible to see the *All American*. We hope so.

Sincerely,
Mark Twain Fifth Graders

Before mailing the letter, Gail enclosed additional material about the World War II project to emphasize the students' interest and enthusiasm in the study.

May 1993

A month later, an answer to their request was received in a letter dated May 6, 1993:

Dear Mrs. Thomas,

Many thanks for your letter of inquiry, for your interest in the education of children about World War II, the part the Liberator played during the war and especially for your interest in the B-24 *All American*. You are to be commended for your efforts in teaching the children of today the ways of life and war fifty years ago.

I'm sorry that we are unable to fill your request for a visit to St. Louis on or about Memorial Day, 1993. The *All American* is on tour in California, Oregon and Washington at present and until the end of June, with Memorial Day booked into San Francisco. Possibly, if a sponsor in the St. Louis area can be found, a visit might be arranged in mid-summer.

Of possible interest to you, we are presently flying the colors of the 456th Bomb Group on the vertical stabilizer of the "All American." *(Fig. 63)* [*Editor's note:* Another coincidence in the story!] This is the bomb group with which George Elliott Rich was flying at the time he was shot down in August of 1944. This bomb group has been the biggest contributor to the *All American* in 1992 and I believe they support a scholarship fund for the children of Cerignola, Italy, the town in which they were based in 1944-45.

We look forward to serving you and the people of the St. Louis area if arrangements can be made.

Figure 63: WWII bombers owned and restored by the Collings Foundation of Stowe, Massachusetts with the B-24 Liberator flying the "colors" of the 456th Bomb Group

Sincerely,
Stuart A. Bemis

P.S. Blechhammer, Germany was a well defended target that sent chills down your spine at briefings. It was making benzene, I believe from coal, to be used as aircraft fuel. This was the target where George Rich went down.

With the information that the *All American* was unable to fly into St. Louis for Memorial Day 1993, Gail put a note on Mr. Bemis' letter to remind herself to consider a fly-in for the following year.

June 1993

A month later, on June 11, 1993 Gail received a phone call from Bob Collings of the Collings Foundation who said the B-24 could come to St. Louis and be at a local airport on July 23rd and 24th. This was the first time a discussion was held as to how expensive a fly-in might be. The B-24 flew in tandem with a B-17 and both planes would need to be involved in an event. The B-17 would cost $4,000 and the B-24 would be $5,000. Additional funds would be needed to cover rental cars and lodging for the crew members of both planes. Mr. Collings said if the Mark Twain fifth-grade students could find corporate sponsors willing to contribute $10,000 to $12,000 a fly-in of the two World War II vintage planes might be possible.

To be able to raise that amount of money seemed daunting to Gail, but if the event could be postponed until the spring of 1995, it would be a fantastic culmination to the four-year World War II study. By waiting two years, corporate sponsors might be found and enough funds raised to permit the planes to come to St. Louis. Profits made by hosting book fairs and poster fairs at the school would be set aside in a special fund for the vintage airplanes.

March 1994

During School year 1993-1994, two book fairs were held along with a poster fair and the fifth graders knew the profits were placed in a special account to be used for the World War II bombers. It was now time to start approaching local businesses, but the students needed an official letter from the Collings Foundation stating the amount required to have an event in St. Louis. On March 16, 1994 they wrote the following to Mr. Collings:

Dear Mr. Collings,

Last year, in April, the Mark Twain fifth graders wrote you a letter saying that they hoped the *All American* would fly to St. Louis to be part of our award winning project called the "Black Suitcase Mystery." It is about a World War II B-24 flyer who was killed on his 50th mission over Germany in 1944.

We heard that you spoke with Mrs. Thomas, our Librarian, last June and discussed the possibility of the *All American* coming to St. Louis if we could get sponsors. We hope the offer still stands. Would it be possible to come in May of 1995? Please note that there would be kids from 5th to 8th grade because Mark Twain students have studied B-24's in World War II since 1991. Plus, we think most of St. Louis and the Illinois area would visit your airplane.

It could be a great-fund raiser for you. You could sell T-shirts, movies about the Liberator, books, trading cards and B-24 airplane models. We would invite all of the St. Louis area to come and see your plane. We would have TV and newspaper coverage because we have already won awards and had the TV people come.

How much money do we need to bring the *All American* to St. Louis? If we hear from you within a few weeks, we'll have enough time to write letters to businesses and start raising money. It would help to know the amount of money we need so we can start asking for sponsors as soon as possible.

Our class would like to see you and the *All American* in St. Louis. We hope you will agree to come.

Sincerely,
Mark Twain Fifth Graders, Class of 1994

Unfortunately, the students did not hear from the Collings Foundation before school ended for the year.

July 1994

During the summer, Gail received a press kit from the Collings Foundation and had a phone conversation with Stuart Bemis. She was told the organization would need a lead time of sixty days for planning events and the 1995 touring schedule was still undetermined, however, May and June were traditionally booked on the west coast. Gail asked that mid-April be considered as a time to visit St. Louis. The fly-in would be a way for the students to commemorate the upcoming 50th Anniversary of "Victory in Europe" which would occur the following month.

Mr. Bemis commented that $11,000 would probably cover the necessary expenses. The planes would cost $ 4,000 for the B-17 and $5,000 for the B-24, plus two hours of fuel inbound and outbound would total an additional $1,600. Crew members would be between six and eight men, so four double rooms at a hotel and one vehicle per aircraft would be needed. He said that hotels and rental car companies often donated free rooms and cars. When approaching corporate businesses, he suggested waiting until early spring to write letters asking for contributions. Often times, stating a short response date was beneficial for obtaining funds.

February 1995

In the middle of February, Mark Twain Principal Jackie Whitworth composed a proposal and prepared to mail copies to major corporations in the St. Louis area. She included a letter of appeal written by the fifth-grade students on February 17, 1995.

Dear Sir,

Hello! We are writing to you from Mark Twain Elementary School in Brentwood, Missouri. Our fifth-grade classes like to learn about past times and we are doing a study/project about World War II. We are learning about the B-24 Liberator Bomber through an award-winning project called the "Black Suitcase Mystery." It is about a man named George Elliott Rich who flew in a Liberator called the *Purple Shaft*. He was stationed in Italy and was killed on his 50th mission way back in 1944.

We are trying to get a B-24 airplane to come to St. Louis. It is called the *All American* and the Collings Foundation spent a great deal of money to fix it up like in World War II times. This is very important to us so we can learn about history long ago. We hope to get the airplane to St. Louis in the middle of April to help commemorate the 50th Anniversary of V-E Day.

But there is one problem. We need to raise $11,000. So, we were wondering if you would donate some of the money. If you help us, we will help you. This is how: you might get your name in the paper or on television because reporters come to our events a lot. It would be good for your business and would mean so much to us.

We need your contribution so we can make this neat airplane come to St. Louis. We can't raise that kind of money by ourselves. So, Mark Twain fifth graders are asking you to donate not a lot, but just as much as you can. We would really appreciate it if you would help support us in this project.

Also, most of the World War II veterans who have heard of us would be extremely glad that you contributed to our cause. Some have been connected with B-24's and would be happy to see one fully restored. There would be Brentwood kids from 5th to 8th grade because Mark Twain students have studied B-24's in World War II since 1991. We think most of the St. Louis and the Illinois area would visit the airplane. Of course, you are invited to see the B-24 as well.

We are hoping that you could help us meet our goal by pledging some money. Thank you for helping Mark Twain students.

Sincerely,
Mark Twain Fifth Graders, Class of 1995

March 1995

Harry Levins, a columnist with the *St. Louis Post Dispatch* newspaper wrote an article in his March 6, 1995 column to help the Mark Twain fifth graders raise the $11,000 for the *All American* visit.

Pupils Find Plane Facts Truly Liberating

The kids in the fifth grade at Mark Twain School in Brentwood need $11,000 in air fare.

They want to pay the expenses that will get two World War II bombers here for an airport visit.

The youngsters have made WWII their special interest—and if they can scrape up the cash, they can touch a part of that era.

What struck me keenly was the type of bomber these youngsters most want to see.

When most of us think of World War II bombers, we think of the legendary B-17 Flying Fortress, which would be one of the two types to fly here. But the fifth graders at Mark Twain care most about the *other* type.

You see, their hero is Sgt. George Elliott Rich, the second cousin of their school librarian, Gail Elliott Thomas.

On Aug. 22, 1944, Rich took off from an air base in Italy for his 50th mission as a waist gunner. This mission was supposed to be his last, and it was. Rich perished over Blechhammer, Germany. He was 22.

His bomber was named the *Purple Shaft*. It was *not* a Fortress. Instead, it was a B-24 Liberator—and that's the piece of aluminum history that the fifth graders want to climb into and crawl around.

Few Americans know that the Liberator could carry more bombs and fly a lot farther than the Fortress. Indeed, almost nobody knows that the United States built more Liberators than Fortresses.

But today, only one flyable Liberator (named *All American*) survives, at the Collings Foundation in Stowe, Mass.

After the war, you see, the Fortress lived on in movies, literature, lore and even your average air show. The Liberator sort of disappeared.

It never got the press the Fortress got. For one thing, the Liberator's high wing and slab sides gave it an ugly-duckling look. For another, it couldn't match the Fortress in altitude and thus tended to get shot down more readily. And scuttlebutt holds that the Liberator was drafty and cold, at least until it got hit, whereupon it burned fiercely.

Still, the Liberator did half the job and got none of the credit. In that way, the Liberator was to the Fortress as the offensive lineman is to the quarterback: the unsung hero.

I learned about that unsung-hero status the hard way two years ago, when I wrote about the European bombing campaign.

That story gave the Fortress the starring role and added that the Liberator "never generated the affection that the Fort inspired, and it flew largely in the war's backwaters."

Wow. The next thing I knew, the letters-to-the-editor column popped and rattled with flak from angry men who had once flown in Liberators. Who says the Liberator was unloved? Me, maybe, but not *them*.

I should have known better. My favorite high-school teacher, Mr. Moore, had flown Liberators in the Pacific in WWII. One day in English class, he read a poem about being a bomber pilot. You write poetry only about the things you love, and if Mr. Moore loved the Lib—well, maybe I should, too.

Anyway, now that the fifth graders at Mark Twain want to see a Lib up close, I hope those ex-Liberator crewmen who sounded off at me now dig into their wallets.

They can get the details from Jackie Whitworth, Mark Twain's principal, at the school, 8636 Litzsinger Road, Brentwood, MO 63144. Contribution deadline is March 15.

Mr. Levin's column was a huge help and donations started to arrive at Mark Twain school, many from former World War II airmen. Gail would often find brief notes attached to the checks. Following are examples of these notes:

Dear Librarian: It is great that a fifth-grade class would be interested in what we did 50 yrs. ago. I wish this could be more but being retired it's not easy. I was an Asst. Eng. and waist gunner on a B-24 and flew 35 missions over Germany and Europe. Tell the 5th graders I appreciate their efforts.

This contribution does not begin to express my appreciation and respect for what you and your school are doing. Thanks and congratulations.

Enclosed is check for $25 in connection with the B-24. Keep up the good work.

Thank you for your efforts, and the involvement of your students, in generating interest surrounding activities during World War II. You and your students deserve much more than our nation's attention. Keep up the good work. Attached check— amount $25.00

This isn't much, but I hope it might help in bringing the *All American* to the St. Louis area. You and your pupils certainly have earned the opportunity to see it.

Gail obtained a list of names and addresses of Missouri residents who were members of the 15th Army Air Force during World War II. She wrote letters and included copies of Mr. Levin's column. Again, contributions came to the school and she received several letters of appreciation.

From Springfield, Missouri:

Dear Ms. Thomas,

I very much appreciate receiving the literature telling of your World War II Commemoration Project. What a super idea! It has long been a concern to many of us who were in World War II that the students of today are being told little of what is obviously an important part of our heritage.

In 1944 I was a 20-year old navigator flying B-24 combat missions out of Italy. The mention of your cousin's last mission over Blechhammer, Germany of Aug. 22, 1944 prompted me to go directly to my flight log for checking. I find that I flew that same day but my target was an ordnance plant in Korneuberg, Austria. Blechhammer was one of the toughest sites targeted by the 15th Air Force. As you are undoubtedly aware, a large oil refinery was located there and the Germans defended it with many anti-aircraft guns. My log indicated that I was there on August 27th, 1944, just five days after your cousin was lost. I was one of the fortunate ones who was able to complete fifty missions. I remained in the service, became a pilot, and spent a combined total of 31 years in the Army Air Corps and the U. S. Air Force.

A check is enclosed to help in your effort to fund the Collings B-24. Incidentally, I was privileged to see and crawl inside the *All American* while attending a reunion celebration in San Diego in 1989. What a thrill it was to once again be in a Liberator!

All the best to you and the students at Mark Twain School! Congratulations to you for all that you have done and are doing!

Sincerely,
Lloyd G. Miller
Colonel, USAF-Retired

From Cape Girardeau, Missouri:

Dear Mrs. Thomas,

Your letter encourages me to believe that your school seeks to present the history of World War II as it actually happened, and in the true context of the world political situation as it then existed. If I am correct in that assumption, I heartily applaud your efforts.

I am alarmed at news reports which seem to indicate a concerted effort to rewrite history texts in ways which tend to excuse the actions of the enemy, and at the same time portray the United States as the aggressor. I object strongly to all such revisions which compromise the factual base of history. We owe no apology to anyone nor any nation for our participation in World War II, or in our prosecution of it to final victory—including the use of nuclear bombs.

Recent shifts in public policy seem to indicate a studied effort to recast some of the happenings of World War II in terms of present day world political climate—for example the modification of plans for the Pearl Harbor observance, the change from "V-J Day" to "Victory in the Pacific," and the Smithsonian's proposed text for the *Enola Gay* exhibit. Things of this nature are an affront to all thoughtful citizens, and particularly so to those—military and civilian alike—who saw their nation through that ordeal.

I note in the newspaper column you sent that your father's cousin was a waist gunner on a B-24 based in Italy. I, too, was based in Italy, near San Pancrazio, a B-24 pilot in the 512th Squadron of the 376th Bomb Group. I well remember the spirit of comradeship which developed among all combat airmen, and even now imparts a sense of personal loss in the death of your kinsman. I am sorry that he had to die.

I was more fortunate. My crew went down in battle on my 25th mission, the December 19, 1943 attack on the Messerschmitt aircraft factory at Augsburg. It was the very first penetration of native German airspace from the south. Nine of our ten crew members parachuted down safely.

Best wishes to you in your efforts to bring the *All American* to St. Louis for your students.

Sincerely,
Daniel P. Rice

Thanks to the publicity generated by Mr. Levin's column, contributions were coming to the school and plans were going forward to have the World War II planes visit the St. Louis area. Then, word was received from the Collings Foundation that the *All American* was unable to schedule a stop in St. Louis during the spring, but they still wanted to be involved in a commemoration and could possibly come sometime in July. Additionally, the price of fuel had increased, so the total amount required would be closer to $12,000.

By this time, of the $12,000 needed for the fly-in, the fifth graders had a total of just over $3,000. Dr. Cleary, school superintendent, suggested that Gail attend a Brentwood Chamber of Commerce breakfast and make another appeal to the local businesses for additional contributions.

The guest speaker at the March 23rd Chamber of Commerce breakfast happened to be Marty Hendin, vice president of marketing for the St. Louis Cardinals Baseball Organization. He made a statement to the audience that the Cardinals wanted to do something for the 50th anniversary of World War II. Gail commented that the fifth graders were $9,000 short of their goal!

Although the Cardinals wouldn't donate that total amount, Marty said a collaboration might be arranged. He suggested that Mark Twain School and the Cardinals Organization join with the local veterans groups in the greater St. Louis area and sell tickets to "Vets Night at the Ball Park." It would be sensational to have the World War II planes fly over Busch Stadium at the beginning of the game. The Cardinals would pledge half of the ticket proceeds toward the cost of the planes. They would also cover the difference if the entire $12,000 wasn't raised. It proved to be a successful partnership and ticket sales continued, with the planned visit of the planes scheduled for July, 1995.

April 1995

With the strong interest in the B-24 Liberator Bombers, Gail was reminded of a World War II veteran who had helped the very first group of fifth graders, back in 1991. Mr. D. H. "Dutch" Borcherding, who served with the 93rd Bomber Group in Europe, was invited back to the school and told the students of his experiences as a German prisoner after his bomber was shot down.

Mr. Borcherding was joined by current-day Air Force officer Walter Ifill from nearby Scott Air Force Base who was also a member of the 93rd BG. Colonel Ifill had volunteered and helped restore a static display of a B-24 Liberator and contributed to the discussion. The two airmen who shared membership in the same bomb group, although fifty years apart, became acquainted in the Mark Twain School library. [*Editor's note:* another coincidence in the Black Suitcase Mystery!]

A week after the visit of the two 93rd Bomb Group airmen, Gail received word that the World War II project had won its fourth national award. The April 23, 1995 *Mid County Journal* printed the following article:

World War II Project Receives National Praise
by Mike Knopfel, Staff writer

Gail Elliott Thomas, a librarian at Mark Twain
Elementary School in Brentwood, loves the past—
particularly World War II. The 50th anniversary year
of World War II will soon be wrapping up and with
it, four years of Thomas' "In Touch with Our Past"
program.

"In Touch with Our Past," which focuses on life in
the 1940s during the war years has received local,
state and national recognition. Thomas received another honor recently when Continental Cablevision
named her as an "Educator of the Year" recipient. She
was one of 13 educators chosen for the award from
among teachers, media specialists and administrators
in more than 700 communities that Continental
serves. The award will be presented April 26-28 in
Washington, D.C.

It was the second time that Thomas received the
"Educator of the Year" honor. She also won it in
1992.

"It's like Gail said at the school board meeting, it's
really nice that it came through at the end of the
program." Said Jackie Whitworth, principal at Mark
Twain. "She got it at the beginning and at the end. It
was a nice closure to it."

Thomas said the "In Touch with Our Past" will not
completely end this year. She said it will continue
as a library research project on genealogy which is
how it began.

Gail was joined by Jackie Whitworth for the ceremonies in Washington and they had the pleasure of reconnecting with Commander Eric Berryman who had helped the students so much the previous year. Eric shared that he and his wife had returned to the areas in Germany that he knew as a child. He said the experiences he shared while at Mark Twain School made him want to revisit his home country.

May 1995

School was still in session on May 8, 1995, which marked the 50th Anniversary of Victory in Europe (V-E) Day. On that day, the Mark Twain fifth graders began a week-long observance of that historic period in America's history. The students also participated in a three day "Electronic Field Trip" broadcast live from Berlin, Germany via CNN's Turner Adventure Learning Program. This program examined the social, political and economic changes that had resulted in the 50 years since "peace broke out."

The televised program allowed students to travel, electronically, to Germany and other European countries to visit people who lived through the trauma of World War II and its aftermath. They relived history and examined war from the viewpoint of the leaders who directed it, the soldiers who fought it, the civilians who lived through it as well as the media who covered it for those at home.

The highlight of the week occurred at 1:30 Friday afternoon (8:30 pm in Germany) when three Mark Twain fifth graders were able to speak directly to Berlin students who, as fifth graders, had grown up in East Germany. *(Fig. 64)* Television viewers around the world heard the Mark Twain students conversing with the German students.

Commemorating the 50th Anniversary of V-E Day was important to the educators and fifth-grade students because it represented the end of their formal study about World War II. On that date, May 8th, Gail had written a letter to each person who had made a contribution to the *All American* fund raiser.

Dear "B-24" Fund Raiser Contributor:

As the current school year nears an end, our students are preparing for our fourth annual "Fifth Graders Focus on the Forties" evening planned for Thursday, May 25 from 6:30-8:00 PM. This has been our traditional way to honor the men and women who helped America during the World War II era. We would like to extend an invitation to you and hope you can attend. Thank you so much for contributing to our B-24 Fund Raiser.

On Monday, May 29, 1995 the following announcement was issued for immediate release by the Public Relations Department of the St. Louis Cardinals Baseball Organization:

Cardinals to Honor Veterans Groups on July 20: Vintage World War II Military Vehicles to Highlight Ceremonies

It is appropriate on this Memorial Day that the Cardinals announce plans for a salute to all veterans commemorating the 50th Anniversary of World War II. The special ceremony is scheduled to take place at Busch Stadium on Thursday, July 20, when the Cardinals play the New York Mets.

Pre-game ceremonies will feature vintage military vehicles and color guards representing all veterans groups in the bi-state area. Former ballplayers will also be among the veterans to be saluted.

Mark Twain Fifth Graders
Speak to Students in Berlin, Germany

By Gail Thomas

May 8, 1945 is commemorated around the world as Victory in Europe Day (V-E Day), marking the end of World War II in Europe. On May 8, 1995 the Mark Twain Fifth Graders began a week-long observation of this historic period in America's history. The students also participated in a three day "Electronic Field Trip" broadcast live from Berlin, Germany via CNN's Turner Adventure Learning Program which examined the social, political and economic changes that have resulted in the 50 years since "peace broke out."

Nate Cole and Mike Schuppan listen as classmate Jaclyn Hodgin speaks to students in Berlin, Germany. All Mark Twain 5th graders participated in an "Electronic Field Trip" commemorating the 50th anniversary of "Victory in Europe" (V-E) Day May 8, 1995.

The students traveled to Germany and other countries in Europe to visit people who lived through the trauma of World War II and its aftermath. They relived history and examined war from the viewpoint of the leaders who directed it, the soldiers who fought it, the civilians who lived through it and the media who covered it for those at home.

The "high-light" of the week occurred at 1:30 Friday afternoon (8:30 p.m. in Germany) when three Mark Twain fifth graders were able to speak directly to Berlin students who, as fifth graders, had grown up in East Germany. Television viewers around the world heard our students conversing with the German students.

The direct phone connections and opportunity to participate in this unique learning experience were the result of Mark Twain's most recent "Cable in the Classroom" Award received for its library research/social studies project "In Touch With Our Past: Fifth Graders Focus on the Forties."

Figure 64: Mark Twain fifth graders talking with students in Berlin, Germany to commemorate the 50th anniversary of Victory in Europe Day May 8, 1995

Funds raised from ticket sales through veterans groups will allow the world's only fully restored and flyable Consolidated B-24 Liberator, the *All American*, to visit the St. Louis area to fly over the stadium to conclude the ceremony.

The project to bring the Liberator to St. Louis has been undertaken by fifth graders at Mark Twain School in Brentwood, Missouri. For the past four years the students have pursued a World War II era research project that deals with the life of their school librarian's relative who was killed in action while on a bombing mission over Germany in 1944. This World War II hero was a radio operator/waist gunner on a B-24 Liberator with the 15th Army Air Force in Italy. Tragically, he was killed on his 50th, and what should have been his last mission.

The fifth graders' World War II project has been recognized at the local, state and national levels, including being cited by President Clinton in his 1994 Memorial Day Speech at Arlington National Cemetery. Mark Twain is mentioned in the United States Congressional Record and was the first elementary school in the entire country to be designated as a World War II Commemorative Community.

Additional proceeds from what will be an annual salute to veterans at the ballpark will benefit John Cochran and Jefferson Barracks VA Hospitals in St. Louis and the Marion, Illinois Veterans Hospital.

Ticket information for the Veterans Salute will be available at a later date.

June 1995

Mr. Hendin's press release prompted several newspapers in the St. Louis area to contact the school and interview Gail and the students. During the month of June the following papers had articles about the project:

June 12, 1995 — *Brentwood Pulse*: "Veterans Night at the Ball Park"

June 14, 1995 — *Chesterfield Journal*: "Groups Collaborate on Tribute"

June 25, 1995 — *County Star Journal*: "Cardinals, Veterans, Librarian to Collaborate on Military Tribute"

On June 14, 1995 Gail received the following fax relating to the *All American*:

Collings Foundation Quick Note

Dear Gail,

This letter is to confirm that the Collings Foundation will be bringing the B-24 *All American* and the B-17 *Nine-O-Nine* to St. Louis July 19 - July 21. We have already started publicizing the stop in our Newsletter to over 4,000 veterans and warbird enthusiasts around the country. The Mark Twain School and the other groups associated with the stop have agreed to endeavor to raise the agreed $12,000 to bring the planes to St. Louis.

We look forward to a very successful event for all involved and a great visit to St. Louis.

Warmest Regards,
David H. Sheppard

July 1995

On July 6, 1995 the St. Louis Cardinals issued another press release and plans were finalized for the long-awaited fly-in of the *All American.*

That press release generated another article by Harry Levins of the St. Louis Post Dispatch who had helped spur contributions in a March column of the paper. On Monday, July 10, 1995 he wrote:

Vintage Bombers Heading This Way

In World War II, many a bomber came home "on a wing and a prayer."

This month, a B-24 and a B-17 will come to St. Louis "on faith" says Jackie Whitworth, principal of Mark Twain School in Brentwood.

The faith is that by then, 180 schoolchildren will have raised the $12,000 that the trip by the bombers will cost.

For the last four years, fifth graders at the school have been involved in a project designed to let them hear about World War II from people who took part in it.

They also hear from school librarian Gail Elliott Thomas, whose cousin, T.Sgt. George Elliott Rich, was killed when his B-24 was shot down. The children wanted to see what a real B-24 looked like—and they'll finally get the chance.

The Collings Foundation of Stow, Mass., has a B-24 (and a B-17, too) that will arrive at Spirit of St. Louis Airport in Chesterfield on the afternoon of July 19. For the next few days, those planes will be open to four years' worth of fifth graders from the school.

The youngsters have raised $4,000, about a third of the cost of flying the planes here. To cover the rest, the Cardinals have joined with veterans groups here to offer a special $6 ticket to the Cardinals-Mets game on the evening of July 20.

Before that evening's game, the bombers will make a low pass over Busch Stadium as part of a "Salute to Veterans."

If the ticket sale raises more than the amount needed to pay for the planes — Whitworth, the principal, says, "They're coming here on faith that the money *will* be raised—the surplus will go to veterans hospitals."

Baseball ticket information is available at any American Legion post. And Whitworth said for a nominal sum, people in the general public can join her fifth graders in climbing through the bombers at Spirit of St. Louis Airport. The planes are expected to fly off about 1 p.m. on July 21.

Gail was thrilled with Mr. Levin's column and promptly wrote a letter to all the Fifth-grade Project Supporters.

10 July 1995

RE: Welcoming Committee for the B-24 Liberator *All American* and Reunion of two World War II Airmen who have not seen each other for 50 years.

Reunion will occur at approximately 2:45 PM on Wednesday, July 19, 1995 at the Spirit of St. Louis Airport, Chesterfield, Missouri.

The two Airmen were eyewitnesses to the explosion of a B-24 Liberator that killed the hero of Mark Twain's 5th Grade Classes, George Elliott Rich.

Dear Fifth Grade Project Supporters:

The enclosed article appeared in today's *St. Louis Post Dispatch*. Two World War II aircrew members who personally knew George will be in St. Louis for the special commemoration events we have planned.

Doug Richards, from Virginia, was the pilot of the *Purple Shaft*. He visited the Mark Twain fifth graders in December, 1991. Dick Verdon, from Michigan, and George trained at the same "radio school" during World War II, but in different classes. The two World War II veterans have corresponded and spoken to each other over the past three years, but have not seen each other for more than 50 years. I hope a reunion will occur in the moments preceding the touch-down of the *All American*.

The newspaper article prompted both Channel 2 and Channel 4 to call me this afternoon. They plan to be at the airport to see the World War II airplanes fly in and hope to be able to speak with the World War II veterans who knew George Elliott Rich.

I hope you will be able to join us a part of a Welcoming Committee when the planes arrive.

For those of you planning to attend the Cardinals baseball game on Thursday, July 20th, please enter by Gate #2. Honor Guards from many Veterans Organizations and World War II military vehicles will be involved as well as a fly-over by the airplanes. Stan Musial and Jack Buck will be there, too!

I hope to see you at the Spirit of St. Louis Airport around 2:45 on Wednesday, July 19th.

The July 16, 1995 issue of the *Mid County Journal* printed the following article about the upcoming reunion of George's former crewmates:

Vintage Memories — Students to See Bombers Land

When two vintage World War II bombers land Wednesday at Spirit of St. Louis Airport in Chesterfield, the experience will be a first-time thrill for many, while calling up 50-year-old memories for others.

The arrival of the B-17 Flying Fortress and B-24 Liberator bombers will be the culmination of a four-year effort by the librarian and students at Mark Twain Elementary School in the Brentwood School District.

Gail Elliott Thomas, the librarian, has taught fifth graders at the school about World War II through studying the genealogy of a relative who was killed in the war.

Thomas' relative, George Elliott Rich, was a radio operator on a B-24 bomber that was shot down during what was to be Rich's final mission.

Thomas began the education project four years ago after finding an old black suitcase containing letters Rich wrote during the war.

Thomas and her students will be present. And they won't be the only ones. Two World War II veterans who saw the explosion of the plane carrying Rich on August 22, 1944 also will be on hand.

Doug Richards of Virginia and Richard Verdon of Michigan will be part of the welcoming party for the two bombers. Richards, a retired Air Force major pilot, and Verdon, a former radio operator, were crewmembers on a bomber flying along-side Rich's B-24 when it was shot down.

Verdon wrote of the incident in a letter he wrote to Richards in 1992. Verdon said in the letter he recalls vividly, . . ."the reflection of flames on the wall of my left side waist position, leaning over to see Rich's airplane peel away."

Richards and Verdon have not seen each other in more than 50 years.

"It's amazing how a little suitcase of old letters has touched so many lives," Thomas said.

The planes will be displayed at the airport Wednesday through Friday. The bombers also will fly over Busch Stadium on Thursday before a St. Louis Cardinals baseball game. The fly-by will be part of Veterans Night at the stadium.

On July 19, 1995 the long anticipated arrival of the *All American* occurred at 3:00 PM. It was not accompanied by the B-17 which had developed engine problems in Illinois. The B-24 Liberator became the star of the show! Perhaps it was fitting that the B-24 received all the glory at the St. Louis fly-in.

Camera crews and reporters from the local affiliates of NBC, CBS and ABC were in attendance to record the reunion of the two World War II crewmembers who had witnessed the B-24 explosion which killed their comrade, George Elliott Rich. *(Fig. 65)*

The *All American* touched down to hundreds of cheers! Visiting dignitaries from the St. Louis region welcomed the crew and numerous World War II veterans clustered around the plane as it was being secured. Once it was opened for touring, they were the first to be invited aboard. *(Fig. 66)*

The next day, tours were available until late afternoon, then the plane prepared to fly over Busch Stadium as a Salute to Veterans. Earlier in the evening, Brentwood students and educators joined the 456th Bomb Group veterans on the field at Busch Stadium to be recognized for their achievement of getting the B-24 Liberator to St. Louis. *(Fig. 67)*

The plane remained at the Spirit of St. Louis Airport until the early afternoon of Friday, July 21st. On the front page of that morning's edition, the *St. Louis Post Dispatch* printed two colored photographs of the *All American* with the headline of "Winging It." *(Fig. 68)*

The caption read:

ABOVE: St. Louis gets a taste of World War II as a vintage B-24 Liberator bomber passes over the riverfront this week, with flight engineer Marti Baker taking in the sights. RIGHT: The plane arrived here

Figure 65: Reunion, 50 years in the making, of WWII pilot Doug Richards and radio-operator/waist gunner Dick Verdon, St. Louis, Missouri July 19, 1995

from Moline, Illinois Airport thanks to the fifth graders at Brentwood's Mark Twain School who have been studying the war. It departs this afternoon from Spirit of St. Louis Airport in Chesterfield. The Collings Foundation of Stow, Mass., owns the plane, named *All American*.

Figure 66: The B-24 Liberator *All American* on the runway at Spirit of St. Louis Airport July 19-21, 1995

The interest generated by the photographs guaranteed a large crowd at the airport for the final morning of tours. Gail was able to talk with many of the Mark Twain students when they toured the plane. Some of their comments are listed below:

> When I first saw the B-24 I was amazed! I thought, "How could this be? A real plane that fought in WWII is still running and I'm seeing it!" I would hate to fly in it or be part of the crew in WWII, though. I thought about how the men were killed fighting for their freedom and we could use this as a memory to remember them!

Figure 67: Pre-game activities during St. Louis Cardinals "Veterans at the Ballpark" event, Busch Stadium July 20, 1995

> When I went walking through the B-24, I could almost hear the echoes of the men yelling and the brave pilot thinking, "My men are the best."

> When I first saw the B-24 I was surprised at its size. It was huge. The tires were bigger than me. It appeared even bigger when I was inside. I was surprised something that big could fly.

> When I first saw the B-24 it was larger than any airplane I had ever seen. I was eager to move the

Figure 68: Front page photos of the B-24 *All American* brought to St. Louis through the efforts of Mark Twain fifth-grade students

controls inside the airplane, but knew I couldn't. It was exciting to go inside the plane. I'll never forget that day I saw the B-24.

I wanted to fire the machine guns and fly the plane. It was a great experience.

I think the B-24 was really fun to see. I really wondered how somebody could fit in the ball turret. You would have to squeeze in the little spot.

The B-24 had a real impact on me. It was a once in a lifetime opportunity.

When I saw the B-24 I was in shock! Wow, I have never seen such a *big* plane. I thought World War II planes were small. I would love to fly a B-24.

The best part was that I got to walk inside the B-24. It was fun walking through the plane. It had a toilet with no privacy. My dad went with me and I wish we could've taken a ride in the plane, but we didn't. We got to see the B-24 take off and it came back around for a fly-by.

Seeing the *All American* was one of the most memorable events, for me, during this *whole* project. It was like meeting one of the most famous and talked-about persons ever.

By early afternoon, the *All American* was once again airborne. With its four engines rumbling, it made one final pass over the crowd before leaving on its next mission. Its visit was an awe-inspiring event that no one associated with the Black Suitcase Mystery could have foreseen four years earlier when the World War II project began. Who could have imagined all the lives that were touched by a "bunch of old letters"?

Fall Semester 1995: Concluding months of the WWII 50th Anniversary Commemoration Events

August - September

When the new school year began, Gail received a letter from the Collings Foundation which had been written on August 29, 1995.

> Dear Ms. Thomas,
>
> Many thanks for the outstanding work performed for the Collings Foundation at our recent stop in St. Louis. It is only through the hard work and dedication of people such as yourself that the Foundation is able to tour these WWII bombers.
>
> Please accept this special issue of *Time Magazine* commemorating V. E. Day, with a four page foldout of the B-24 as a token of our appreciation for a job well done and for the time you spent to assure that the public got a chance to view and tour the aircraft.
>
> We look forward to bringing the planes into areas where we can expect the type of cooperation we got from you and your volunteers. We hope to see you again in the near future.
>
> Sincerely,
> Bob Collings
> Collings Foundation

The August—September issue of *Lifestyles of the 50 Plus* newspaper featured the St. Louis Cardinals Baseball organization and the visit of the *All American* B-24 Liberator.

Busch Stadium's 1st Annual Salute to All Veterans

July 20th a multifaceted ceremony honoring all of the veterans who have served our country, especially those who served in World War II was held at the Busch Stadium.

Funds raised from ticket sales through veterans groups allowed the world's only restored and flyable B-24 Liberator, the *All American*, to visit the St. Louis area and fly over the stadium to conclude the ceremonies.

The project to bring the Liberator to St. Louis was undertaken by fifth graders at Mark Twain School in Brentwood, Missouri. For the past four years the students have pursued a World War II Era Research Project that deals with the life of their school librarian's cousin, George Rich, who was killed in action while on a bombing mission over Germany in 1944.

This World War II hero was a radio operator/waist gunner on a B-24 Liberator with the 15th Army Air Force in Italy. Tragically he was killed on his 50th and what should have been his last mission.

Some of the fifth graders, along with their librarian joined in the ceremonies at the Stadium. Two World War II veterans who witnessed the death of George Rich also joined the students on the stadium field. After more than 50 years, these members of the

456th bomb group had a reunion at the Spirit of St. Louis Airport yesterday when the world's only fully restored B-24 arrived in town.

Pilot Doug Richards flew with Rich for almost a year before that fateful mission. He came from Blacksburg, Virginia to participate in the "Salute to All Veterans" activities at Busch Stadium.

Dick Verdon, radio operator on B-24's, traveled from Kalamazoo, Michigan to meet his former pilot and join the students and veterans in the World War II commemorative events.

Another World War II veteran, also from Kalamazoo, Michigan is June Wandrey Mann. June Wandrey recorded World War II from ambulance and tent as her surgical mobile unit followed the infantry. She spoke to the students last December when she was in St. Louis to commemorate the 50th Anniversary of the Battle of the Bulge.

There were also special vehicles on display at the stadium. These included vintage vehicles from the Armed Forces Museum, a U.S. Army Duck converted to a Navy Vessel and a 40 and 8 locomotive train. Veteran group officials were also on the field.

Jefferson Barracks and Marion, Illinois Veterans Hospitals will receive all of the proceeds from this first and all future salutes in Busch Stadium.

Two Hall of Famers who were representing all of the baseball players and baseball personnel who took part in World War II were Red Schoendienst and Jack Buck. Representative from the American Legion presented special awards. Jack received a Purple Heart after being wounded in the war. Stan Musial was also presented an award which Red and Jack accepted for him.

The sound of the B-24 rumbled overhead as the ceremonies concluded and an all-service Color Guard marched onto the field.

November

The official end of the 50th Anniversary of World War II Commemorative events occurred on Veterans Day, November 11, 1995. On November 16, 1995 the Governor of the State of Missouri wrote the following letter.

Ms. Gail Thomas, Librarian
Chairman, 50th Anniversary of World War II Commemoration Committee
Mark Twain Elementary School
8636 Litzsinger Road
Brentwood, MO 63144

Dear Ms. Thomas:

Mr. James Whitfield, Chairman of the State of Missouri's 50th Anniversary of World War II Commemoration Committee has shared with me the reports that you have been sending the Committee. I am impressed with the thoroughness of your activities and with the knowledge of World War II which you have been able to impart to your students. I commend you and your students for both your patriotism and your initiative in conducting these activities.

Very truly yours,
Mel Carnahan

Governor Carnahan's letter, written shortly after Veterans Day, 1995 acknowledged the end of the official 50th Anniversary of World War II Commemorative Events. The Mark Twain students and staff realized that, by hosting their World War II Night on December 6, 1991 to commemorate the 50th Anniversary of Pearl Harbor's bombing, they had been involved with commemoration events during the entire official four year period, 1991-1995.

PRESENT DAY

Present Day

The events described on the previous pages occurred nearly twenty-five years ago. Looking back, as I reread George's letters to his mother and remembered the amazing experiences that developed from the contents of the Black Suitcase, my chief sensation is one of astonishment. No one involved with the four year World War II study could have anticipated the twists and turns that occurred as the "Black Suitcase Mystery" unfolded.

My heart ached for my great-aunt Hazel as I imagined her life separated from the son she so dearly loved. To have had George's company for just one brief week after a thirteen year absence, only to lose him entirely on his 50th and what should have been his last combat mission, had to have been devastating.

My last visit with Hazel occurred the summer of 1977, just before my husband was transferred to Germany. At the time, Hazel would have been seventy-three years old. During that visit, we spent several hours discussing the Elliott family history and looking at old photographs. Hazel did not reveal the Black Suitcase, nor did she say anything about her son George.

However, she did show me a purple dress hanging in her closet, with a Purple Heart decoration pinned to the bodice. She said she wanted to be buried wearing that dress! As a thirty-year-old, I found the discussion about her funeral a bit morbid and remember quickly changing the subject. Not until recently, after reading one of Wanda's 1944 letters, did I realize that Wanda originally had both of George's Purple Heart awards. She had mailed one to Hazel as a keepsake. It was Hazel's desire to take that last remaining bond with her son, to her grave. Hazel died July 25, 1979, thirty-five years after George's death.

When Wanda and I visited the Summer Street Cemetery in 1992, a shiny new gravestone was in place. The stone was inscribed, "Wanda B. Rich Dilley, Separated by War, Reunited by Death." Wanda told me that it gave her great peace of mind to know that she would be buried next to George. She said, "George was my romantic love. You don't replace a romantic love unless you're lucky. There are things I've never forgotten about our marriage."

There is one final irony in this story. In 1993 I spent a week at the Air Force Research Center in Montgomery, Alabama. I wanted to read the official records of George's 456th Bomb Group and its combat history in Italy. I was also curious about George's original group. He was assigned to the 382nd Bomb Group in Pocatello, Idaho when he and Wanda married in 1943. It was while in the 382nd Bomb Group that George forged the pass to get into town to see his bride. He was apprehended at the gate, lost his stripes, some of his pay, and was confined to quarters for a month. During that thirty-day period, the 382nd Bomb Group shipped out and George was eventually reassigned to the 456th Bomb Group.

George served with the 456th Bomb Group on bases in Idaho, Nebraska, Utah, California, Cerignola, Italy and

Stornara, Italy. The group was one of six B-24 groups that served with the Fifteenth Air Force, taking part in the strategic bombing campaign as well as supporting the troops in Italy and the south of France. The 456th Bomb Group received two Distinguished Unit Citations for its strategic bombing.

George's original group, the 382nd Bomb Group was stationed at bases in Utah, Arizona, Idaho, California, Texas and Kansas. It was equipped with the B-24 Liberator and served as a home-based training unit. The 382nd Bomb Group did not see combat.

One is left to speculate if the "Black Suitcase Mystery" might have had a different ending had George not forged a pass and been apprehended at the gate. That one action, totally uncharacteristic of George's usual behavior, had tragic consequences!

Although George Elliott Rich died in 1944, he continued to serve his country during the 50th Anniversary of World War II. By reading George's letters to his mother, ten-year-old students were given a glimpse into the life and times of a pivotal point in our nation's history. They were able to see that history is not the written account of events that don't matter anymore. They understood that what real people did in the past did indeed touch their lives.

December 7, 2016 will mark the official beginning of the 75th Anniversary of World War II. I am reminded of George's 1942 postcard to his mother, sent the day he finished his Basic Training which in essence said, "On my way, but don't know where." I wonder what lies ahead for the Black Suitcase and its many-faceted story. I do not yet know the answer, but I believe this incredible tale will endure.

The Black Suitcase and George's postcard, which expressed a typical military sentiment: "On my way, but don't know where."

AUTHOR BIO

Gail Elliott (Thomas) Downs is a retired elementary school educator with thirty-seven years' experience as a classroom teacher, reading specialist and school librarian. She grew up in an Army family and became an Army wife, but had little knowledge of the 15th Army Air Corps activity during World War II. As the Black Suitcase Mystery project unfolded, Gail learned, right along with her fifth-grade students, about World War II aviation and the missions flown by B-24 Liberator bomber crews.

Gail currently resides on the Oregon Coast and is available to give presentations about the Black Suitcase Mystery. Contact may be made by emailing Gail at:

blacksuitcasemystery@gmail.com.

ACKNOWLEDGMENTS

*W*ithout the commitment of the following people, the Black Suitcase Mystery project would not have been possible. Mark Twain Elementary School principal, Jackie Whitworth, who approved the proposal of an extended study of American life during the World War II era. Fifth-grade language arts teacher, Leslie Brann, who guided the students on a daily basis. The enthusiastic fifth graders in the classes of 1991-1995 who solved the initial "mystery," then went forward and made subsequent discoveries none of us could have imagined when the project began.

The *Black Suitcase Mystery* in printed form was made possible with the help of Donna Rhoda who contributed countless hours of work scanning photographs, reformatting rough drafts and brainstorming ideas with me. Krysten Polvado used her graphic-artist skills to design the front and back covers. Matt and Nanette graciously offered their editing and design expertise which brought the manuscript to completion.

My most sincere thanks to each and every one of you.